TRIPLANES

A Pictorial History of the World's Triplanes and Multiplanes

D1511610

Peter M. Bowers and Ernest R. McDowell

Motorbooks International
Publishers & Wholesalers ®

First published in 1993 by Motorbooks International Publishers & Wholesalers, PO Box 2, 729 Prospect Avenue, Osceola, WI 54020 USA

Motorbooks International is a certified trademark, registered with the United States Patent Office

The information in this book is true and complete to the best of our knowledge. All recommendations are made without any guarantee on the part of the author or Publisher, who also disclaim any liability incurred in connection with the use of this data or specific details

We recognize that some words, model names and designations, for example, mentioned herein are the property of the trademark holder. We use them for identification purposes only. This is not an official publication

Motorbooks International books are also available at discounts in bulk quantity for industrial or sales-promotional use. For details write to Special Sales Manager at the Publisher's address

Library of Congress Cataloging-in-Publication Data

McDowell, Ernest R.
    Triplanes / Ernest R. McDowell, Peter M. Bowers.
      p. cm.
    Includes index.
    ISBN 0-87938-614-2
    1. Triplanes—History.   I. Bowers, Peter M.   II. Title.
TL684.5.M38   1993
629.133′343—dc20   93-6994
                              CIP

On the front cover: This Fokker Dr.I replica is painted in the bright red color made famous by the Red Baron in World War I. *H. G. Frautschy*

On the back cover: Top left, the Paulhan triplane. *Bowers Collection*. Lower left, the Lloyd 40.08 bomber of 1916. *Bowers Collection*. Top right, the Euler Type II triplane. *Heinz J. Nowarra Collection*. Center right, the Austin Osprey triplane. *Bowers Collection*. Lower right, the NBLR-1, commonly called the Barling Bomber. *US Army*

Printed and bound in the United States of America

Contents

Foreword

Why Triplanes?

And why not? For the first few years of human flight on rigid wings in this century, there was no standard arrangement of wings for flying machines. By the time the Wright brothers were established as aviators, distinction had been made between two basic types of heavier-than-air aircraft: unpowered gliders and their powered equivalents, aeroplanes.

As yet there were no definitive terms for configurations such as monoplane, biplane, triplane, quadruplane, and so on. The early pioneers who acted alone and with limited access to the progress of others in the field went their own way. No doubt some figured if one wing was good two must be better, and three, four, or more even better yet. One pioneer went so far as to design an aeroplane that resembled a Venetian blind. Some aeroplanes had their pitch controls ahead of the wing, after the Wright Flyer design, in what later became known as the canard configuration. Others had the tailplanes behind the wing, feeling that this method was good enough for birds. And still others had tandem sets of wings. Until shortly before World War I, little effort was made to differentiate types among the various designs; all were just aeroplanes in that era of "cut-and-try" designs. However, primary distinction by the number of mainplanes (wings) was pretty well established.

Although the first successful aeroplane (airplane hereafter, to conform to current usage) that flew, the Wright Flyer, was a biplane; the triplane arrangement had been considered by others, and a few models had actually been constructed and flown in pre-Wright years.

Why three wings instead of one, two, or even four or more? Given the strength of materials versus weight in those days, the main advantage of the triplane was its ability to accommodate a great amount of wing area over a shorter wingspan than was possible with the monoplane or biplane arrangement. This greatly simplified the structural requirements for building the one or two wings of sufficient span to contain the wing area deemed necessary by the designer. Historically, three wings have been the optimum arrangement for large lifting areas. It is notable that none of the famous "giant" airplanes of history have been quadruplanes, though several have been triplanes.

Another advantage of the triplane, proven in war, was the improved maneuverability of the fighter plane over the biplane type. Triplanes required a much shorter takeoff run as well.

Of course, three wings produced more aerodynamic drag than did one or two wings, but in the years prior to World War I, airplanes were such high-drag designs that the added drag of another wing was almost insignificant.

The definitive term triplane was solidly entrenched in the aviation vocabulary by 1909, although it sometimes appeared in print as "tri-plane." The word has generally been used to identify an airplane or glider with three wings of nearly equal size, arranged vertically one above the other. In pre-World War I years some three-wing airplanes were what today would be called triple tandem monoplanes, that is, with their three wings laid out longitudinally. Three wings, whatever their arrangement, constitute a triplane in the eyes of the authors, so they have been included in this book.

Further, since it is such a short, logical, and interesting step up from three wings to four or more, these too have been included under the designation of multiplanes.

This book presents an overall survey of triplanes and multiwing plane configurations from the 1868 model built by John Stringfellow to the present-day boom in the World War I replica building. However, it does not claim to cover every triplane or multiplane design ever built. The authors cast a wide net, but undoubtedly some "fish" may have gotten away. A few examples did surface which no amount of research can identify, and those are presented as "mystery ships" in the hope that some knowledgeable reader can identify them.

This book is divided into several distinct historical periods by chapter, with the appropriate triplane chapter for each period followed by a chapter on contemporary multiplanes. Because of the large number of triplanes developed during World War I, that period is covered by two chapters, one on single-seat fighters, and one on larger models. Although some airplanes that were under construction as 1918 World War I prototypes were not completed until after the war, they still are included as World War I types.

Others begun in 1918 or earlier but not completed until later are presented as postwar models. Some World War I triplanes with significant postwar developments appear in both wartime and postwar chapters.

Most airplanes described in each chapter are listed alphabetically by the manufacturer's name, regardless of nationality or chronological order. A few, however, appear out of order to help the flow of the narrative.

Acknowledgments

An undertaking of this broad scope is simply not possible without the enthusiastic support and cooperation of a large number of people. Aviation historians, photographers, collectors, other authors, and the staff members of museums and official archives throughout the world have been most helpful. These individuals and organizations are gratefully acknowledged in alphabetical order:

Col. J. Ward Boyce
J. M. Bruce
Caproni Museum, Italy
Alberto Casirati
Fred C. Dickey, Jr.
Frederick G. Freeman
Chuck Graham
William Green
Peter M. Grosz
Imperial War Museum, London
Alex Imrie
Bert Kemp
Ted Koston
Lars Knudsen
Art Krieger
William T. Larkins
Musee Royal De L'Armee
    Et D'Histoire Militaire,
    Belgium E. A. Jacobs

Nils-Arne Nilsson
Heinz J. Nowarra
Leonard E. Opdyke
Alain Pelletier
Sten Persson
Renaud Pouge
Walter Redfern
Boardman C. Reed
Brian Shadbolt
Shirley Smith-Haskell
Smithsonian Institution
    Washington, D.C.
F. Gordon Swanborough
John Underwood
Verkehrshaus Luzern
    Musee Suisse des Transports,
    Switzerland

Photographs from the collections of deceased individuals are not listed here since they were not direct contributors to this book. The postmortem credit lines acknowledge their past contributions to aviation history and the authors' appreciation for use of their works.

Photo Credits

The use of a large number of photographs of very old airplanes, as included in this book, creates a serious problem of assigning proper credit to the individual photographs. In most cases, these photographs are not available from the originating organizations. However, copies are available in several private and public archives, each of which will apply its own credit line when releasing a copy for publication.

The authors have tried to be as accurate as possible when crediting photos, considering the present availability of the material. Photos obtained from the Imperial War Museum in London, for example, are credited to that organization even though other archives may contain the same photos. Others are credited to the specific collections or individuals from whom they were obtained, and are presumed to still be available from those sources.

It does little good to credit a photo to a manufacturer that has been out of existence for seventy-five or more years and whose files no longer exist. When original prints of such photos are in the authors' private collections, they are credited to those collections even though copies may still be available from other sources.

Chapter 1

The Pioneer Years: 1842-1914

Although the first successful heavier-than-air powered flight was achieved by the Wright brothers in December 1903, the seeds of their success had been sown as far back as the mid-nineteenth century. Many scientific minds had tackled the problem, and while they might not have built successful flying machines, many of their ideas were carried forward and resulted in successful designs.

Some workable ideas were committed to paper, and a number of small models and even human-size gliders were built and allegedly flown. But the major obstacle to progress was the lack of a suitable powerplant. Powerplant technology had a long way to go before it could make the dream of powered flight possible.

The so-called standard configuration of the modern airplane, a monoplane driven by a propeller, with pitch and directional controls in the rear, and a wheeled undercarriage (tricycle, yet), appeared in the form of William Samuel Henson's published concept of a flying machine that he called Aeriel in March of 1843. In addition to establishing the modern configuration of the airplane, Aeriel also contributed the basic modern wing structure of spanwise spars and chordwise ribs, the whole covered with an airtight cloth.

A contemporary scientist, Sir George Cayley, disapproved of the monoplane wing of Aeriel and suggested that the 150ft wingspan be reduced by incorporating the same amount of area in what he termed a "Three Decker," with each wing being 8–10ft (2.4–3.1m) above the other to allow room for the free passage of air between them.

Nothing came of this recommendation either by Henson or Cayley. It remained for an associate of Henson, John Stringfellow, to combine the ideas. In 1868 Stringfellow built a three-wing variant of *Aeriel* in model form. It had a wing area of 36sq-ft (3.3sq-m) and was powered by a small steam engine that drove two propellers, and weighed only 12 pounds less the powerplant. The arrangement of its three wings established the triplane configuration as used by most subsequent triplane builders. Incidentally, the term Three Decker as used by Cayley is the current German word for triplane, *Dreidecker*.

Thanks to the late nineteenth century builders of small, weight-controlled gliders, humans finally got off

the ground on rigid wings. The major contribution of the Wright brothers to heavier-than-air flight was their perfection of a workable three-axis mechanical control system.

After the success of the Wright brothers, a flood of new designs appeared in both the United States and Europe. Initially most of these were biplanes, but monoplanes came on strong by 1909, and triplanes were not at all uncommon. However, none of the triplane designs achieved what could be considered production status, most being experimentals or simply biplane designs with an extra wing added.

Astra Triplane

In spite of the Astra's cumbersome size, the airplane was quite modern in appearance considering the time frame in which it first appeared. The fuselage was encased in metal sheeting and the framework was made from strong steel tubing, giving it an empty weight of 1,650lb (750kg) with a useful payload of 880lb (400kg). The powerplant was an eight-cylinder Renault, which one source lists as producing 65hp while another claims it achieved a maximum of 74hp.

Some interesting features of the design were its dual tail wheels, and its four landing gear rubber-tired disk wheels which closely resembled automobile tires. A span of 39.36ft (12m) gave it a 484.9sq-ft (45sq-m) wing area. The bottom wing was located very close to the ground, requiring that it be operated from a level runway with no obstructions. The ailerons were free hanging, but would be forced upward during the takeoff run and become a part of the wing surfaces. There were none on the bottom wing. Each lower wing tip had a semicircular skid to protect the wing tips during takeoff and landing. A unique feature was that the main landing gear was set into V-shaped cutouts in the lower wing.

The Astra triplane was test flown successfully by Marcel Goffin in late 1910.

Battaille Triplane

The Battaille triplane was designed by Cesar Battaille, a Belgian, in 1911. A single-seat, single-engine plane, with its wings staggered rearward, the Battaille was powered by a 42hp Gregoire engine. Battaille used a unique method to ensure the three wings were

Test pilot Marcel Goffin checking the fuel stopcock prior to a flight in the Astra triplane. Note the V-shaped cutouts for the main gear wheels. The fuel tanks often were placed high enough to allow for gravity feed. The clear panel just above the inboard right wheel gave the pilot a view of the ground upon landing. Courtesy Alain Pelletier

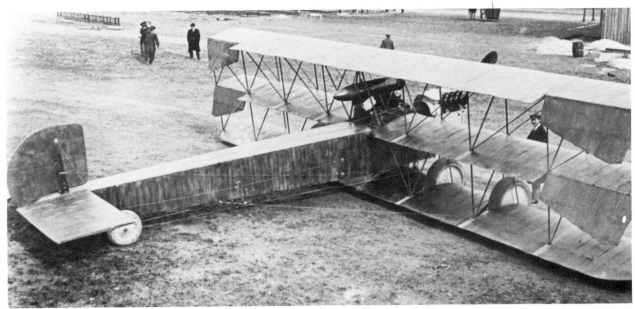

View of the V-shaped cutouts in the bottom wing which accommodate the main gear wheels. A slab rudder and elevator were used. Courtesy Alain Pelletier

equidistant by placing the midpoint of the center wing at the center of a circle, and the midpoints of the top and bottom wings on the circle's circumference. This gave a 45deg rearward stagger. The wingspan was 34.4ft (10.5m), giving a 260.8sq-ft (24.2sq-m) wing area. The bottom wing was set below the fuselage. Wings and tail surfaces were fabric covered; the forward portion of the fuselage was wood sheathed. A wooden propeller was fitted and the undercarriage had both wheels and skids. Craftsmanship was excellent throughout, resulting in a sturdy airplane whose appearance was ahead of its time.

In 1972 the Battaille family donated the plane to the Musee Royal De L'Armee in Brussels, where it is carefully being restored to be placed on exhibit in tribute to Cesar Battaille, one of aviation's true pioneers.

Bokor Triplane

The Bokor was an American venture and was credited with being the third American aircraft design to leave the ground. While it made several short flights, none were significant. The Bokor was powered by a four-cylinder 34hp Thomas engine with a 4.0in (102.6mm) bore, a Livingston radiator, and a number of specialized fittings. The engine drove two propellers with an 8ft (2.4m) diameter via a chain drive.

The plane was a pusher type. It used four bicycle wheels on a square base as its landing gear, though these occasionally were replaced by runners. Steering was accomplished by means of a 14x2.5ft (4.3x0.8m) biplane elevator in front; a vertical rudder was mounted behind the tail, which consisted of two pairs of triangular planes set at a dihedral angle on a frame extending from the middle wing and from about 2ft (0.6m) below the top wing. The wings had flexible

In-flight photo showing the dual tail wheels, with the ailerons in normal position held by the slipstream. The arrangement of the gear made for good stability on the ground and it would seem to be almost impossible to ground loop the Astra. Courtesy Alain Pelletier

From this view, the scant clearance between the lower wing and the ground is very apparent. The view port panel has been removed, and you can see into the cockpit. While the struts and bracings are clearly visible, the rigging wires are not. Courtesy Alain Pelletier

French pilot Francois Chassagne at the controls of the Battaille triplane, about to call out "Contact" as an assistant   *gets set to spin the propeller. Belgian Musse Royal De L'Armee*

edges with a gap between the top and center wing of 5ft (1.5m), and between the middle and bottom of 6ft (1.8m). The wings were 6.5ft (2.0m) wide, and the middle and bottom wing were curved, but the top wing was flat. Small, flat planes were mounted at the rear of the middle and bottom wing. Wingspan was only 26ft (7.9m), but the wing area was 580sq-ft (53.8sq-m). Gross weight including the aviator totaled 1,181lb (534.4kg).

Borgnis-de Savignon I Triplane

Borgnis of the Bousson-Borgnis and Borgnis-Devordes partnerships teamed up with another part-

Nose view showing the undercarriage and engine mountings. The square-tipped wooden propeller was close coupled to the engine. The steel-tubing undercarriage featured both wheels and skids, resulting in a sturdy design. Belgian Musse Royal De L'Armee

Closeup of the Battaille's linen-covered tail surfaces. Considering the time period involved, these are a departure from standard practice. Belgian Musse Royal De L'Armee

Ribbing structure details show a well-engineered and carefully constructed wing that provided both strength and lightness. The wing surfaces were covered with doped linen. Belgian Musse Royal De L'Armee

The wooden sheathing covering the forward fuselage and the lower wing attachment bars can be seen in this photo. Note the control wheel. Belgian Musse Royal De L'Armee

Since the wooden nose of the plane ended just aft of the engine, the purpose of the wooden rectangle is unclear. It may be a temporary barrier to protect the engine area. Various *fittings were added to strengthen the plane.* Belgian Musse Royal De L'Armee

The Bousson-Borgnis pusher triplane leaves no doubt as to who the designers may have been: their names are embla- *zoned on what appears to be a plane to add stability to the creation.* Bowers Collection

ner, the Comte de Savignon, to build a triplane. They had another in the works as well, embodying slight variations, though nothing seems to have come of it.

Type I was built in 1908. It was a large, fragile-looking aircraft. The body was built of steel tubing and was mounted on a set of four wheels like an automobile. The wings were curved planes, which were reduced in depths at the tips. It had ailerons mounted on the center wing but no tail, and a single-plane elevator placed forward on a level with the bottom wing. Steering in the horizontal plane was by means of the ailerons only. A 28hp six-cylinder engine drove an 8ft (2.4m) diameter pusher-style propeller which was chain driven and geared down. The wingspan was 47.75ft (14.56m), wing area 861sq-ft (79.95sq-m), and the gross weight was 1,257lb (571.4kg). The three wings were of equal length and chord.

The triplane was constructed to use a track for takeoffs, but no record has been found to indicate it was ever flown.

Bousson-Borgnis Triplane

The Bousson-Borgnis triplane was designed and built in France.

The Bousson-Borgnis plane was powered by a Buchet 34hp engine driving a pusher propeller. The wings and front-mounted elevator were flimsy cloth-covered items mounted on a metal-tubing fuselage. There was no rudder. A large trapezoid of cloth was mounted vertically on the fuselage to provide lateral stability and also as a billboard to advertise the names of the designer team, featuring them in large lettering. The fuselage was mounted on a tricycle undercarriage, with the engine mounted on a platform over the wheels.

Burchard Triplane

The Austrian triplane was odd, almost a Rube Goldberg type construction. It had a main section of triple wings, with triplane sections on either side set slightly lower than the main section; these acted as stabilizers. The wings were set four feet apart. Steering was by means of an ordinary motor car steering wheel. There was a horizontal rudder in front, with two semicircular balancers. A cellule consisting of two horizontal planes and two vertical rudders mounted behind the wings. Two bicycle wheels were mounted in tandem, while a pair of small supporting wheels under the main plain ends provided balance.

There is no record of whether the Burchard was successfully flown.

Curtiss Triplanes

Glenn Hammond Curtiss was invited to join the Aerial Experiment Association (AEA) by Dr. Alexander Graham Bell because of Curtiss' proven ability as an engine designer. Curtiss had earned the title of Fastest Man on Wheels while riding a motorcycle powered by one of his own engines—at a world record of 136.3mph (219.8km/h). Another reason for Curtiss' appointment was that his plant at Hammondsport, New York, had the necessary facilities to build the AEA planned airplanes. While there, Curtiss contributed to joint airplane design efforts and won the first leg (of three) of the Scientific American Trophy with a controlled powered flight in excess of 0.62mi (1km) on July 4, 1908.

Eighteen months after it was formed, the AEA was disbanded. It had designed four aircraft, all of which flew, including Curtiss' own June Bug. Curtiss next formed a partnership with Augustus M. Herring, a former associate of Octave Chanute (an early experimenter with gliders). Together they produced the Golden Flier which they sold to the Aeronautic Society of New York for $5,000, and the Rheims Racer that Curtiss flew to victory in the first Gordon Bennett Cup air race at Rheims, France. As a result of a dispute over the prize money, the Curtiss-Herring association ended in April of 1910. Curtiss went on to found the

Curtiss Motor Company on December 19, 1911, and became the leading developer of new airplane designs in the United States as well as the principal manufacturer. (The Wright brothers had ceased airplane development due to litigation tie-ups in defense of their patents.)

Curtiss' first triplane, built in 1911, was not designed as such. It was simply a stock Curtiss Model D pusher biplane, which was given additional wing area the easiest way—by adding a third wing above the other two. When flown as a land plane, the third wing's span differed from the span of the other two. Later, when converted to a seaplane, the span was increased

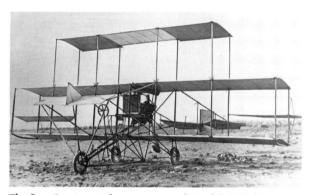

The first Curtiss triplane was a stock Model D biplane fitted with a short third wing to provide additional lifting surface. Bowers Collection

When the Curtiss triplane was fitted with floats in 1911, the upper wing was lengthened to provide still more lift to carry the added weight of the floats. Notice the wing-tip skids. Paul Matt Collection

The Curtiss triplane with wing-tip floats instead of skids. This was a much more practical application. The photo was taken at North Island, San Diego, California, in 1911. Paul Matt Collection

to add area needed to provide the extra lift to handle the extra weight of the pontoon.

Specifications:

Powerplant, 50hp Curtiss Model O water-cooled V-8 engine; wingspan 26.25ft (8.0m); wing area 354.4sq-ft (32.9sq-m).

De Bolatoff Triplane

Construction of the de Bolatoff triplane was begun by the French firm Voisin, at Mourmelon, France, in 1908. Serge de Bolatoff, a Russian prince with a burning desire to fly, had a hand in the design and thus it was considered a Russo-French effort. When development progressed at a slower pace than he anticipated, de Bolatoff decided to switch his operation to Brooklands, England, where the triplane was finally completed near the end of 1913.

The de Bolatoff had a 120hp four-cylinder Panhard engine to drive the two-bladed propeller. Taxiing trials were held at Brooklands in November of 1913, but the machine was damaged on the ground by a gust of wind. The damage was eventually repaired and the plane was moved to Reigate Aerodrome, where a final attempt was made to fly it in 1914. The attempt failed, however, when the left front undercarriage collapsed during a ground loop.

The airplane looked like two large box kites fastened together. The tail wheel was augmented by a pair of short skids. Other skids were mounted on the wing tips, and on the tips of the extra-large triplane tail. The tail was so large it almost could have qualified the aircraft as a tandem triplane, but it was designed as a triplane. Serge de Bolatoff's name was emblazoned along the fuselage sides in large lettering.

The Ellehammer triplane being inspected by some aviation fans in Denmark. Later the top and middle wings were clipped, and still later the middle wing was removed. Hans Ellehammer via Lars Knudsen

Ellehammer Triplane

Jacob Christian Hansen "Hans" Ellehammer was born in Denmark in 1871, the son of a carpenter. His natural mechanical aptitude led to an education as a watchmaker. In 1895, the twenty-four-year-old Ellehammer went into business for himself by opening a mechanical workshop in Copenhagen, producing and repairing motorbikes. While the business flourished in the summer months, it was naturally slow during the winter. So, Ellehammer decided to try his hand at inventing a flying machine.

Although Ellehammer had had no contact with other inventors in the field, he built his first plane in 1905. It was designed to fly around in circles while attached to a pole. Later, he designed and built a full-scale triplane using an engine of his own design. For the triplane he used steel tubing (bicycle tubing), mahogany, and linen to cover the wings, elevator, and tail wheel which was also used as the rudder and operated by a steering wheel. The elevator was run by a pendulum stabilizer seat which operated by pushing the seat forward to climb and backward to descend. There was no stabilizer on the plane's transverse axis. Initially, the aircraft was reported to have been powered by Ellehammer's three-cylinder air-cooled radial engine of 18hp. Later he replaced this with a more powerful engine also of his design, a six-cylinder air-cooled radial type producing 30hp. The two-bladed propeller was replaced by a four-bladed oar type.

As other improvements and modifications continued, the top and middle wings were clipped and squared off. Finally Ellehammer removed the middle wing, concluding that it offered no appreciable advantage. In January 1908, he flew it as a biplane. Satisfied with its performance, in July he took it to Kiel, Germany, to compete for a prize of 5,000 marks, which he won with an 11sec flight. This was the first free flight over German soil.

Ellehammer built his last airplane in 1912 and overall made close to 200 flights in his various airplanes. Meanwhile he continued to work on his helicopter design, which he completed in that same year. Though he died in 1946, the company he founded is still in existence in Copenhagen but now manufactures fire extinguishers for ships and general industrial use.

Escobedo Triplane

A Brazilian inventor named Escobedo planned to produce a triplane transport in 1917, and even went so far as to take out a patent in Brazil as well as other countries. His idea was to distribute the weight over almost the entire fuselage and thus be able to carry as many as forty passengers.

The plane envisioned by Escobedo would be lighted by electricity. A cabin 6.6ft (2.0m) and 8.2ft (2.5m) would be installed in the nose with room for an observer, pilot, wireless equipment, and large fuel tanks. Two 500hp engines would drive two pusher and two tractor propellers. The top wing was to be the longest, with the other wings decreasing in size. A biplane tail would be attached to the long, boxlike fuselage. Ailerons would provide for lateral stability. The landing gear would consist of two pairs of wheels and a pair of forward-mounted skids. Escobedo hoped to attain a speed of 93mph (150km/h).

Specifications:

Length 42.6ft (13.0m); wing area 2,392.2sq-ft (222sq-m); stabilizer 431.0sq-ft (40sq-m); total area 2,823.3sq-ft (262 sq-m).

Euler Triplanes

August Euler, of Frankfurt-am-Main, was Germany's first licensed pilot. He got into airplane manufacturing very early by obtaining a license to build French Voisin designs. Before the start of World War I the Euler Flugmaschinen Werke produced a variety of aircraft, most based on existing designs of others. The company enjoyed good sales for the times.

Among those produced were two triplane designs. In 1911, Euler adapted a Farman-type pusher biplane to a triplane by fitting it with three slightly smaller wings. The lower wing was placed well below where the lower wing of the biplane was attached to the pod's lower longeron. The center wing was attached to the upper longeron, and the upper wing was farther above

The first Euler triplane was essentially a modified French biplane design. Notice that both ailerons are down; they floated upward to fair with the wing at flying speed. Bowers Collection

The 1911 Euler triplane fitted with a float for use as an amphibian, on exhibit at the 1912 Aero Show. The inscription on the nose reads Euler No. 3, and the one under the cockpit reads Euler Flugmaschinen Werke Frankfurt-am-Main. Bowers Collection

The Euler amphibian triplane of 1912. The wing panels are made up of individual short sections. Courtesy of Franz Selinger

the pod than on the biplane. This aircraft model was also demonstrated as an amphibian, with a single wooden float between the wheels, and cylindrical sheet-metal auxiliary floats under the lower wing tips. A German-built Gnome (built under license by Oberursel) rotary engine served as the powerplant.

In 1912 Euler introduced an original design, a considerably larger pusher triplane amphibian flying boat with retractable landing gear. The aircraft was powered by a 100hp French Anzani ten-cylinder twin-row air-cooled radial engine.

Facielli Triplane

Designed by Signor Facielli of Turin, Italy, circa 1908, this triplane was a bit heavy for its time, largely due to its 441lb (200.5kg) SPA (*Societa Piemontese Automobili*) motor which produced 75hp. It was a four-cylinder horizontal type with two pistons to each cylinder. The pistons on each side drove a crankshaft which in turn drove the two pusher propellers.

Wingspan of the two top wings reached 32ft 8in (10.0m), with a chord of 5.5ft (1.7m). The middle wing was open in the center to accommodate the aeronaut, while the top wing was full span. The bottom wing was shorter than the other two. Two stabilizer planes were mounted in front of the plane, and there was a tail at the rear with a vertical rudder. Gross weight was 1,102lb (500.9kg), not including the aeronaut. The plane had a normal two-wheel landing gear.

The Facielli was the first Italian triplane of note.

Farman I Triplane (Voisin type)

Henri Farman, a French pilot, teamed up with the Voisin brothers to produce the Farman I, a biplane that made its first flight in 1907. This airplane was the first in Europe to make a controlled turn. Early on, Farman had set a number of records for endurance and distance in this airplane as well as others. The Farman I was converted to a triplane and sold to an Austrian syndicate, but when it failed to live up to their expectations, they donated it to the Austrian Army, which converted it back to a biplane.

The Farman I was a larger plane with a wingspan of 42ft 8in (13.0m), and 645sq-ft (59.9sq-m) of lifting area (including the tail surfaces). The wings had a chord of 5.75ft (1.75m), and the planes were set 5ft (1.5m) apart. Total weight with pilot added up to 1,231lb (559.5kg). The fuselage was 38ft (11.6m) long by 6.5ft (2.0m) wide. The main gear consisted of two wheels in front and a tail wheel. A 50hp eight-cylinder, air-cooled Antoinette weighing 209lb (95kg) provided the power to drive its 7ft (2.1m) diameter propeller. Steering was accomplished by two wooden horizontal rudders in front on each side of the fuselage, and a vertical rudder inside the box tail. The original Farman I had a top speed of 35mph (56.5km/h), which was reduced when it was converted to a triplane.

Goupy Triplane

Ambroise Goupy designed his own Model II biplane in 1908, which was built by Louis Bleriot. With the biplane a success, Goupy next created a triplane design to be built by Gabriel Voisin, who also contributed to the design work. During a period of several months that year, from September 5 to December 7, Goupy made four successful test flights at Issy, France. His best flight was only 490ft (149.4m), but it was

Ground crew adjusting the rigging wires on the Farman I prior to a flight at Issy, France. The aileron is down, but in *flight the slipstream forced it up level to the wing.* Bowers Collection

enough to give the Goupy the honor of being the first triplane to actually fly.

The Goupy was powered by an eight-cylinder 50hp Renault engine. Gross weight was 1,105lb (500kg). The wingspan of 24.6ft (7.5m) gave the plane a compact appearance, and its tail, fabric-covered wings, and fuselage gave it a more modern look. The elevator was set in the middle of the box-kite-like tail. Side curtains enclosed the mainplanes and a rudder projected behind the box tail.

Grade Triplane

The Grade triplane was the first German-made airplane piloted by a German to fly over its homeland. It covered a few yards at Magdeburg on January 12, 1909.

The Grade strongly resembled the Ellehammer triplane of Denmark, which was the first airplane to fly in Germany. The Grade's design featured a tricycle undercarriage and a cruciform tail mounted at the rear. The top wing was straight, while the other two curved slightly at the ends. The wings had approximately a 2ft (0.6m) gap between them. The engine was mounted on the middle wing and drove a tractor propeller.

The Grade triplane made several successful flights.

Hammond Triplane

E. V. Hammond designed and built a triplane that was tested at Brooklands, England, by C. Howard Pixton in February of 1911. Pixton had been granted Aviator's Certificate No. 50 at Brooklands on January 24, 1911, while flying an A. V. Roe triplane.

The Hammond design featured a pair of tractor propellers belt driven from the engine, a fore-mounted elevator on twin booms, twin rudders, and a horizontal tail plane with twin booms mounted. Very broad chord ailerons were attached to the upper wing. A four-wheeled undercarriage and wing-tip skids gave a good measure of ground control on takeoff and landing.

Mackensie–Hughes Triplane

The Britannia was a triplane designed for E.S.B. Mackensie-Hughes by A. W. Smith of Barking, England, in 1910. A J.A.P. (J. A. Prestwich) four-cylinder engine drove two propellers that were phased 90deg apart, and their blades intermeshed where their swept disks overlapped. The center wing had a broad chord, and the top and bottom wings had a much narrower chord. Lateral control was handled by ailerons on the center wing. Both the wings and triple horizontal tail surfaces were staggered rearward. The weird appearance gave it the nickname of "The Staircase." The landing gear had both skids and double-wheel trucks.

The Britannia was tested on July 9, 1910.

The Goupy I being pulled into position for a test flight at Issy, France, in the summer of 1908. It flew 490ft (149.4m). Bowers Collection

The Paulhan being positioned for a test flight. The fuselage nacelle closely resembles a motorcycle sidecar. The number under the left wing is unexplained. Bowers Collection

Three "supervisors" watch one worker adjust a strut while another works on the engine. What appears to be a rudder is attached to the right rear boom. Bowers Collection

Specifications:
Span 23ft (7.0m); wing area 250sq-ft (23.2sq-m); empty weight 600lb (272.7kg).

Molesworth Triplane

In August of 1910 the Mackensie-Hughes triplane was redesigned and rebuilt by H. B. Molesworth. Keeping the name Britannia, Molesworth installed an E. N. V. Model F engine in the nose position, and a two-bladed propeller with direct-drive to overcome the heating and power loss on the original plane. He also replaced the triplane tail with a new monoplane tail mounted on the top of the upper longerons, and a rear-mounted rudder.

Louis Paulhan Triplane

The Paulhan triplane was a pusher-type aircraft powered by a 75hp Renault engine. A four-bladed propeller was attached to the short nacelle-type fuselage which was suspended between the middle and lower wings. It had a four-wheeled Farman-type undercarriage, with a skid between each set of wheels. Each skid had a pair of small wheels to protect the pilot in case of the nose tipping over. Twin booms extended to both front and rear of the plane. The horizontal tail plane was attached to the booms in the rear, and the elevator plane was attached in front.

The Paulhan triplane was designed to carry a pilot and two passengers. It grossed out at 1,550lb (704.5kg). The plane was completed in October of 1911, in time for the French Military Trials.

Pischoff–Koechlin Triplane

Pischoff and Koechlin teamed up during 1905–1906 to build a triplane of very unusual design based on the box-kite format. The pilot lay in a prone position behind the propeller. Tubing encircled his shoulders, and he was protected from the propeller by another circle of tubing. One wing was positioned beneath the pilot, and another under the engine. The two wings were separated by a gap. A third wing was positioned on top of the plane and ran the length of the aircraft. The undercarriage was a four-wheel type, with two wheels in front and two at the rear. Since the plane had no rudder, elevators, or ailerons, there was no positive control other than in a straight line forward.

A. V. Roe Triplanes

Alliott Verdon Roe's first attempt at designing a triplane, as partner with engine designer J. A. Prestwich, failed since they could not get a 35hp engine.

On Roe's second attempt he was forced to use wood instead of the light-gauge steel tubing that he wanted to use. He also had to settle for the heavy J.A.P. 9hp engine. The fuselage was made up of three longerons and cross struts and wire bracing which formed a triangular girder. A triplane tail unit was used: bicycle wheels for the main gear, with a smaller wheel under the tail. A four-bladed air screw, 9ft (2.7m) in diameter, mounted 3ft (0.9m) above the engine on a pulley driven by chains or belts. The outer 6ft (1.8m) of the wings folded back to allow for easier transporting and storage.

Roe flew 100ft (30.5m) in Roe I on July 13, 1909. The aircraft is now on display at the Science Museum in London.

Roe built a second triplane almost identical to the first, but with a 20hp J.A.P. four-cylinder air-cooled engine. This plane differed from the first in having a tail skid instead of the wheel, and was tapered toward the rear so far as the fuselage section was concerned. The span was 20ft (6.1m), length was 23ft (7.0m), and wing area stretched to 285sq-ft (26.5m). The tail planes spanned 10ft (3.1m) with 35sq-ft (3.3sq-m) of surface. Weight was 300lb (136.4kg) empty and 450lb (204.6kg) loaded. Range was 1,500ft (457.3m) at a speed of 25mph (40.25km/h).

Roe II was named *Mercury* and was about the same size as Roe I. However, it had a 35hp Green four-cylinder, water-cooled engine and a two-bladed wooden, adjustable pitch air screw. Two spiral-tube radiators were built into the fuselage to provide cooling. The fuselage was made of ash and covered with Pegamoid fabric.

A rigid triangular undercarriage was fitted with a two-wheel axle secured by rubber shock-absorbing cord. The overall structure was superior to the Roe I, and was a bit larger having a span of 26ft (7.9m), the same 23ft (7.0m) length, and a slightly smaller wing area of 280sq-ft (26.0sq-m). But the loaded weight was increased to 550lb (250kg), and the maximum speed to 40mph (64.4km/h). The Roe II prototype was destroyed in a fire on a freighttrain, when sparks from the engine ignited it while it was being shipped to the Blackpool Flying Meeting on July 27, 1910.

The Roe III triplane prototype was a two-seat aircraft similar to the Roe II, but differed by having the mainplanes fixed to the fuselage, and bottom wing shortened to a span of 20ft (6.1m). The rudder was increased in size, while the triplane lifting tail was retained. Five-foot ailerons with a 2ft (0.6m) chord were hinged to the rear spar of the top wing and slightly inset. A Farman-type undercarriage with twin skids and four wheels was fitted for extra strength. The 35hp J.A.P. eight-cylinder vee air-cooled engine provided more power than on the Roe II. Since the plane had a tendency to overheat, flights were limited to about twenty minutes. First flight of the Roe III was made on June 21, 1910. Flying the plane himself, Roe passed the Royal Aero Club tests and was awarded Aviator's Certificate No. 18 on July 26.

Three other specimens of the Roe III were built. They were similar but had the top wingspan increased to 31ft (9.5m), and the ailerons were now placed on the midwing and the fuselage covered around the cockpit. One prototype was destroyed in the same train fire as Roe II, however. Roe sold another to the Harvard University Aeronautical Society. He had cracked up

The second version of Roe I. The tail skid, tapered fuselage, and cylindrical fuel tank all differed from the first example. Also, the undercarriage had more struts. This plane made its first flight on December 9, 1909. A four-cylinder JAP 20hp engine improved its performance. Truman C. Weaver Collection

the third Roe III, but repaired it and took it to the United States for the Boston Aviation Meeting scheduled for September 2, 1911. Again, bad luck dogged him and he crashed the aircraft. He then took his engine and mounted it in the Harvard triplane, and made several hops before wrecking it on September 15.

Avro number 1 powered by a 24hp Antoinette engine was a wooden structure with paper-covered fuselage. It had a span of 20ft (6.1m), was 23ft (7.0m) long, and had a 320sq-ft (29.7sq-m) wing area. It weighed 200lb (90.9kg) empty and 400lb (181.8kg) loaded. The craft was named Bulls Eye. Flight International

The Roe III had a gross weight of 750lb (340.9kg), with the upper wingspan reaching 31ft (9.5m) and the lowest 20ft (6.1m). Wing area was 287sq-ft (26.6sq-m), and the tail plane area was 75sq-ft (7.0sq-m). Four Roe IIIs were built.

Roe's last triplane design was the Roe IV which had been completed in September 1910. It was a single-seater similar to the others, powered by a 35hp Green water-cooled engine with the radiator mounted in the center section gap. The shorter bottom wing was further reduced by a narrower wing chord. The triplane tail was replaced by a monoplane type equipped with movable elevators. It reverted to the four-wheeled undercarriage. The upper span was 32ft (9.8m), lower 20ft (6.1m), and gross weight 650lb (294.1kg). Wing area had increased to 294sq-ft (27.3sq-m), and the fuselage was lengthened to 34ft (10.4m) (after one of the many crashes).

The Roe IV was cracked up many times by the students at the Avro Flying School. It was finally scrapped in August of 1911.

Scott Triplane

The Scott triplane was built by J. F. Scott of Chicago, and tested by the US Army in 1909. The design consisted of two front mainplanes 144sq-ft (13.4sq-m) in area, with three rear wings totaling 414sq-ft (38.4sq-m). These produced a lifting factor of 560sq-ft (52.0sq-m). The front planes were divided in the center to allow for independent warping, while the rear planes were adjustable to any angle to suit the speed.

The Roe IV was a great structural and aerodynamic advancement over its predecessors. This photo is of a fairly accurate replica built for the film Those Magnificent Men and Their Flying Machines. *The fuel tank on the upper wing, and the engine and propeller differ from the original, though.* Courtesy Greenborough Associates

Maximum wingspan was 26.25ft (8.0m). Two chain-driven propellers were mounted in a manner similar to the Wright brothers' machine. The aircraft had a total weight of 650lb (294.1kg).

No record of the Scott triplane exists in the files of the Chicago Historical Society. However, the fact that it was built in Lawrenceburg, Indiana, may account for the discrepancy.

Stringfellow Triplane

At nearly age seventy, John Stringfellow returned to the United Kingdom in 1868—after a twenty-year stay in the United States—to display a steam-powered triplane at the historic first exhibition of the British Aeronautical Society in London. Stringfellow's purpose was to resolve the main criticism made by Sir George Cayley in 1843 of the Aerial Steam Carriage with which he had been connected. This model also failed to fly.

Cayley had sent a boy a few feet into the air in 1849, but not in free flight. He had used a full-size airplane designed as the triplane he had recommended at the time of the William Samuel Henson controversy six years before while he was trying to develop a hot-air engine, but did not try it in the glider. He fitted the glider with flappers in which the pilot was, in effect, to row it to sustain flight. Cayley reported: "A boy of about ten years of age was floated off the ground for several yards on descending the hill, and also for about the same space by some persons pulling the apparatus against a slight breeze by means of a rope."

In 1853, using a full-size machine which he called his New Flyer, Cayley and his assistants moved to the east side of the deep dale behind Brompton Hall, his country home. He put his coachman in the car, again equipped with handles to work the flappers and levers to brake the undercarriage wheels. The machine was pulled down the hill until it became airborne. It sailed across the valley, well stabilized because of Cayley's previous trimming, and was not immediately affected by the coachman's frenzied manipulation of the flappers. After a flight of about 1,500ft (457.3m), not as smooth as hoped for, it hit the other side of the dale and flipped over. Everyone rushed to aid the coachman from the debris. Old Cayley, no longer spry, took his time, and when they freed the coachman and helped him to his feet, he cupped his hands to shout across the valley his reaction to this moment in history, "Please, Sir George, I wish to give you notice, I was hired to drive, and not to fly."

Cayley's Old Flyer (Boy Carrier) of 1849 had a 10ft (3.01m) wingspan, overall length of 20ft (6.1m) and stood 20ft (6.1m) high. A tricycle landing gear mounted directly to the aircraft.

Vanniman Triplane

The Vanniman triplane was the center of a controversy in 1908 when a photo of it flying was later proven to be fake.

It was an unusual design in that everything was in front of the wings. The horizontal rudder for steering was placed forward of the top and middle wing. The

John Stringfellow's model triplane was first displayed in the Crystal Palace in London during the British Aeronautical Society's exhibition in 1868. It had a wing area of 28sq-ft (2.6sq-m) and was powered by a $\frac{1}{3}$hp engine that weighed only 35lb (15.9kg). Brian Shadbolt Collection

The pilot wearing a derby looks like he is facing backwards due to the Vanniman's unusual design. The rail tracks that the airplane operated from can be seen both behind and in front of it. The fuel tank on the midwing must have been a worry to the pilot in case of a crash. Bowers Collection

elevator was also placed forward on a twin boom with skids attached. Side tips were added later to the middle wing. It was a pusher type, with a four-wheel undercarriage. The wheels were fitted on a track which was used to ensure that the plane took off in a straight line.

Wullschleger and Peier Triplane

Fritz Wullschleger and Albert Peier, pioneer Swiss aircraft designers, took a radical approach to wing design that resulted in an almost complete oval shape. The bottom wing was curved upward and the top wing was curved downward. The outer struts joined these wings together, while the middle wing tips also curved downward. The middle wing was longer than the other two.

The plane's engine mount and undercarriage were quite similar to a Bleriot design. A five-cylinder air-cooled radial engine provided the power. The fuselage was covered with fabric. A cruciform tail with rudder and elevators gave the aircraft a more modern look. The upper wing panels were in three sections, the middle wing in four sections, and the bottom wing in three. While the airplane *looked* good, it never flew.

Fritz Wullschleger and Albert Peier posed with their airplane in 1913. Judging from their expressions, they still had not managed to get it off the ground. Swiss Transport Museum, Verkehrshaus Luzern

Chapter 2

Pioneer-Era Multiplanes

While the majority of pioneer-era flying machines were biplanes, following the lead of the Wright brothers, with a smaller but substantial number of monoplanes and a sprinkling of triplanes, some inventors opted for designs with more than three wings. In some cases they simply added one or more conventional wings to an existing design. Others elected to try a more radical approach, and sought a way to obtain the necessary amount of lifting surface to get the plane off the ground. Given the technology of the day and the strength of the materials available, it was easier to get the desired lift from *several* wings rather than from a long-span *single* wing or even from the biplane wings.

Some of these planes constructed with more than three wings, which we choose to call multiplanes, fit conventional designations like quadruplane or quintuplane, tandem-wing or canard. Others defy classification by present-day standards.

Tandem Wings

The conventional airplane as we know it today evolved between 1903 and 1913. This put the wing or wings in front, and the tail surfaces for pitch and yaw control at the end of a tapered box-like fuselage. Some of the earliest designers chose the tandem-wing configuration with wings of equal size at opposite ends of the fuselage sharing the flight loads in proportion to their size. Tandem-wing designs persisted into World War I and experienced a minor revival in the mid-1930s, and again in the 1970s and 1980s.

Although it had only two wings, the tandem-wing Langley Aerodrome of 1903 is included here because it is not only the most well known of the tandems, but it is also the design to which all other tandem-wing types must be compared. The tandem-wings are presented here in chronological rather than alphabetical order.

Langley Aerodrome

Professor Samuel P. Langley, a scientist and Secretary of the Smithsonian Institution in Washington, D.C., experimented with the heavier-than-air problem by successfully flying a steam-powered model in 1896 and another with a gasoline-powered engine in 1903.

In that year he built a full-scale Aerodrome that was to be launched by catapult from the top of a houseboat on the Potomac River. Attempts on October 2 and December 8, 1903, both ended in crashes that terminated the experiments. In 1914 Glenn Curtiss, seeking to invalidate the Wright brothers' control system patents by proving prior use, resurrected the old Aerodrome, modified it considerably for conventional takeoff on pontoons, and flew it successfully.

The layout of the Aerodrome was interesting. In addition to the two wings, a cruciform tail was mounted behind the rear wing for elevation (pitch) and directional (yaw) control. There was no provision for lateral (roll) control, however. The stability benefits of a high dihedral angle for wings was well known at this time, so an angle of seven degrees was used.

Specifications:

Powerplant, 50hp Manley water-cooled radial engine; span 48ft 5in (14.8m); length 52ft 5in (16.0m); total wing area 1,040sq-ft (96.5sq-m); gross weight 750lb (340.9kg).

Kress Triple Tandem

Although it had only three wings, the 1914 Austrian Kress flying boat is included in this chapter because it was not a triplane in the accepted sense: its wings were not mounted in a vertical rise.

Wilhelm Kress also tackled the problems of powered flight in a remarkable parallel to Langley's work by flying rubber-band-powered models in 1898 and 1899. Except for the third wing, these were similar to Langley's models in layout.

A full-scale example with 366sq-ft (34.0sq-m) of wing area was built with a 24hp Daimler gasoline engine in the hull driving two pusher propellers behind the center wing. The first and only test was made in October of 1901, but the plane rolled over in the water. Since there were no wing-tip floats and the hull was too narrow to provide lateral stability, the result was inevitable.

It is just as well that the Kress did not fly. It had no provision for roll control and no dihedral to give lateral stability. The flimsy wing structure could have deflected under load, if not failed completely.

Jones Tandem

It is hard to determine just how many wings the Jones machine of 1905 actually had. The rear wings were clearly two separate units, but the closed structure in front is questionable as to whether it was a single unit or two, which would make it a four-winger but certainly not a conventional quadruplane.

Charles Oliver Jones built his tandem in Dayton, Ohio, in 1905 and powered it with a 25hp air-cooled gasoline engine manufactured by Glenn Curtiss. The plane was too heavy and underpowered to taxi more than 10mph (16.1km/h), but even if it could have achieved flying speed it could not have flown because of its flat wings—no airfoil wing sections were incorporated into the design. The one notable contribution that Jones did make to subsequent designs through Curtiss, however, was the wheeled landing gear for rolling takeoffs and landings. As mentioned, Langley had used a catapult, and the Wright brothers had used a dolly and rails for takeoff and skids for landing.

Dufaux Triple Tandem

Credit for making the first aerial flight in Switzerland goes to the Dufaux aircraft of 1908. It dispensed

The Langley Aerodrome of 1903, as restored by Glenn Curtiss in 1914, with its original Manley engine amidship driving two pusher propellers. Bowers Collection

The Aerodrome as further modified by Curtiss, using an 80hp Curtiss engine to drive a single tractor propeller through an extension shaft. Bowers Collection

Der Tandem Dreidecker, the first Swiss-built flying machine ready for a test flight in 1909 with Dufaux at the controls. He seems lost amidst all of the wings and rigging wires. Note the windmill-type propellers and the landing gear. Swiss Transport Museum

The unsuccessful Austrian Kress tandem flying boat of 1901. View shows the flimsy wing construction, the flat-bottom boat type hull, engine mount, and pusher propellers. Bowers Collection

The Jones tandem triplane was the first airplane that Glenn Curtiss took an active interest in because it ran one of his engines. The man in the center is Charles Oliver Jones, the first person to lose his life while flying in a dirigible, in September 1908. Glenn Curtiss is on the left, and Leonard Waters is on the right. Bowers Collection

with using ailerons for lateral stability by using a high dihedral, and further followed the Langley pattern by combining the lifting and pitch-control surface at the extreme rear in a biplane unit.

The Dufaux was one of the highest-powered airplanes of its time. It had a 120hp PS-Dufaux motor enclosed in a complete nacelle like a dirigible, with two very large propellers mounted behind the front set of wings. The engine was water cooled; the cooling water was forced through the cylinder jackets, which were corrugated to increase the cooling effect. Air was then forced through the pistons to cool them. This was necessary because of explosions occurring on both faces of the pistons. The pistons and rods were hollowed out to allow air circulation which was provided by a rotary air blower operating at a speed of 5000rpm.

The aircraft was fitted with tricycle landing gear which, by this time, was fairly common. The Dufaux was still flying in 1909.

Specifications:
Span 26ft 2in (8.0m); wing area 646sq-ft (60.0sq-m).

1907–1908 Voisins

True tandem-wing airplanes had major lifting surfaces at each end of the structure, often with an auxiliary set of surfaces for pitch and/or yaw control. This could be either behind the wings as on the Langley, or ahead of them, as on the French Farman built by Voisin.

The Voisin exemplifies how some tandem-wing designs devolved from true tandems, with major lift on each end, to more acceptable conventional designs. The biplane rear wings contributed a major share of the lift; slightly less lift, however, because of their shorter span. Succeeding designs kept shortening the rear wings and moving the center of gravity forward so that the rear surfaces, still with airfoil sections, generated only enough lift to balance the plane longitudinally. Since such "lifting tails" introduced severe trim problems with changes in air speed, the lift function was soon deleted by the use of flat or symmetrical sections and then adding hinged elevators for pitch control.

Specifications:
Powerplant, 50hp Antoinette engine; span 33.5ft (10.2m); gross weight 1,145lb (518.1kg).

Other highly original multiple configurations were plentiful in the pioneer era, along with more conservative approaches to aircraft design that merely stacked additional wings on fairly standard fuselages. Here are a few such designs:

AEA Cygnet

Alexander Graham Bell, inventor of the telephone, became interested in the possibility of powered flight and thus formed the Aerial Experiment Association (AEA) at Baddeck, Nova Scotia, Canada, on October 1, 1907. One of the AEA's earliest experiments involved a passenger-carrying kite designed by Bell and named Cygnet.

The Cygnet departed from the established box-kite construction by having a wing built up of a framework containing hundreds of small tetrahedrons, small flat surfaces arranged in vees to provide the lift for the tetrahedron kite.

The Cygnet, which had no means of control for the pilot, made one successful flight when towed into the wind by a boat. However, it was destroyed after coming down in the water while being towed. Because of lack of control, the AEA pursued other lines of development for its flying machine experiments.

Bell persisted, however, and built a larger-powered version named Cygnet II. This model had a wingspan of over 40ft (12.2m), was fitted with a biplane canard elevator, and a Curtiss V-8 engine behind the

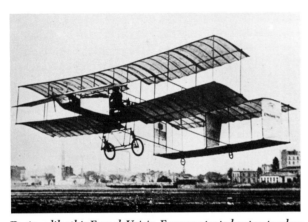

Designs like this French Voisin-Farman started out as tandem biplanes with pitch control through a forward (canard) elevator. The span of the rear wings gradually decreased until they became a true tail and took over the pitch control function. Heinz J. Nowarra Collection

wing as a pusher. The pilot was located ahead of the wing.

Cygnet II was tested on the ice at Baddeck on February 22 and 24, and again on March 15, but it was too heavy to fly with the available power. In March of 1912 a cut-down version, Cygnet III—powered with a 70hp Gnome rotary engine, and fitted with a monoplane canard elevator, and a rudder and fixed stabilizer behind the wing—made a series of straightahead flights on the ice. The purpose was not so much to advance aviation, but was a sentimental gesture to prove that the venerable Bell's unique wing would actually work.

D'Ecquevilly Multiplane

The 1908 French d'Ecquevilly multiplane, identified only as that, is certainly one of the most unusual would-be aircraft configurations ever built. The designer, the Marquis d'Ecquevilly, must have felt that if one wing was good, and two were better, then why not go all the way and use *seven*? With its flat airfoils and no visible tail surfaces or means of operating some of the wing panels as ailerons, there is no way this contraption could have been flown successfully. It did make one significant contribution to subsequent airplane design, however: its structure was fashioned from steel tubing.

The d'Ecquevilly incorporated a rather common practice of the time, that of turning the propeller located remotely from the engine through belts or chains to reduce the speed of the propeller relative to the engine's speed. Designers did not fully understand propeller theory; they believed that all the work was done by the back of the propeller blade, like that of an

1909 MAR 15

Dr. Alexander Graham Bell's Cygnet. The powered version of his tetrahedral kite, named Cygnet II, was tested on the ice at

Baddeck, Nova Scotia, on March 15, 1909, but it was too underpowered to fly. Bowers Collection

oar. However, some aircraft did fly successfully with paddle propellers such as this. Early on, propellers were thought of as air screws.

Specifications:

Powerplant, 8hp air-cooled Anzani; span 16ft 5in (5.0m); length 6ft 6.75in (2.0m); wing area 269sq-ft (25.0sq-m); empty weight 309lb (140.5kg)

Sellers Quadruplane

American inventor and aviator Matthew B. Sellers started flying in 1909 with a quadruplane glider that featured an unusually high degree of stagger. He later flew it successfully with an 8hp engine mounted between the second and third wings driving a tractor propeller.

Sellers continued to develop his quadruplane configuration by marrying the wings to a conventional fuselage, landing gear, and powerplant. He still retained a high degree of originality in the example shown. The fixed horizontal tail served only as a stabilizer. Pitch control came from altering the angel of attack of the top wing, while lateral control was provided by the second wing from the top. The separate panels moved differentially as ailerons.

Vedovilli Multiplane

Vedovilli was a well-known manufacturer of electrical appliances when he decided to become involved in aeronautics. His brain child, or perhaps his brain storm would be a more apt phrase, was given the name Le Fanthom (The Ghost). Although it went through possibly four modifications and was tested over a three-year period at Issy-les-Moulineaux (now the Paris Heliport), it never flew. An eye-witness account stated, "The mastodon rolled two or three hundred meters, at a speed of three kilometers, then just stopped with an 'exhausted' engine." The last variant literally fell apart during a taxi run, in 1911. That ended the career of the monstrosity.

The first Vedovilli weighed 1,657lb (750kg) but had a wing area of only 538.8sq-ft (50sq-m). It was made of wood, probably hickory which is easy to form when heated. A huge rudder was mounted behind the cockpit, which was shaped like a "stem" and was the first enclosed cockpit using panels of mica or celluloid fixed on a wooden frame.

A four-cylinder inline water-cooled engine was located behind the cockpit. The two-part radiator was mounted on each side of the motor and shaped like a wing plane on top of the fuselage. The four wings were constructed of a single stringer and forty stiffening

The Marquis d'Ecquevilly built this machine in France in 1908. He is standing in the center. The multiplane's wing cellule was made up of twelve planes. Five "winglets" on each *side were topped by a pair of full-span wings. The paddle-bladed propeller was common at the time. Bowers Collection*

ribs, and were covered by linen on both surfaces. The wings were mounted on two horizontal swivels which permitted the pilot to increase the incidence, or to bank by pulling on control wires. The first plane had a single pusher propeller; later, Vedovilli tried to switch to twin propellers. The new version was given a high vertical fin and a front wheel, and a fixed gear was added later.

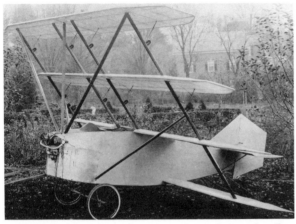

A later development of the original Gordon and Sellers quadruplane, designed by Matthew B. Sellers of Baltimore, Maryland, in 1908. The original was powered by a two-cylinder, four-cycle opposed air-cooled engine. The plane weighed only 23lb (10.4kg). Bowers Collection

This profile view shows the cleanness of the Sellers design. Wing area was 200sq-ft (18.6sq-m). The engine was a Dutheil-Chalmers. Air speed was a low 23mph (37.0km/h). Note the large tail skid. Bowers Collection

The heavy stagger of the four wings was common to the original glider and all subsequent powered versions. Gross weight was 78lb (35.3kg). Sellers' ambition was to develop the lightest flying machine in the world. Notice the strut arrangement and bracings. This may have been the first successful "midget airplane" developed anywhere. Bowers Collection

Barton-Rawson Hydro-Multiplane

In 1905 at St. Helen's on the Isle of Wight, Dr. F. A. Barton, his son Dudley, and F. L. Rawson built an all-bamboo floatplane with multiple sets of wings. On September 26, 1905, tests were conducted with the engine installed by towing it behind a motor launch on a tow rope, like a kite. During the tests the ropes kept breaking and eventually resulted in a crash in which the plane turned over in the water. Although it was salvageable, the designers finally abandoned the aircraft since they were unable to obtain an engine weighing under 500lb (227.3kg).

The multiplane's floats were 20ft (6.1m) long, 10in (25.4cm) wide, and 4in (10.2cm) deep. The plan was to use a 7ft (2.1m) propeller which would be driven by a 35hp motor. Span was 34ft (10.4m), length 36ft (11.0m), height 9ft (2.7m), and wing area 1,200sq-ft (111.4sq-m). Empty weight sans engine and propeller was only 240lb (109.1kg).

Batson Flying House Multiwing

Capt. Arlington Batson, who had designed a successful monoplane at Maidstone, England, in 1910, set his sights on creating the Flying House in 1913. His dream was to make a transatlantic flight.

To call the good captain an eccentric is an understatement. He actually built a "house" instead of a fuselage, and fitted no less than twelve wings on it. The fuselage contained a sitting room and bedrooms for his crew. Apparently, he believed in traveling in comfort; no doubt a bar was included. A ladder led up to the house which had four normal-size windows plus a door. The aircraft appears to have had a pusher and puller engine mount and attached floats. Wings consisted of four upper wings in both front and rear, and four lower wings mounted in the middle. Twin rudders were attached to the tail.

Obviously the Batson Flying House never flew, so the good captain was spared the embarrassment of a crash.

Dwight and Lund's Tandem Quadruplane

Dwight and Lund, a pair of aircraft designers with a local reputation of being "fast promoters," built a huge tandem quadruplane in McCormick hangar number 3 during the winter of 1911–1912. McCormick, a member of the farm machinery family, became interested in aviation and sponsored many flying events and assisted aircraft designers.

This quadruplane stood about 15ft (4.6m) or more high. Its eight wings were all of equal span and had no stagger. A pair of wheels was mounted below each set of tandem wings. The wings were joined by a trellis-like structure that extended from the bottom of each lower wing to the top of each third wing. A pair of trapezoids were installed between the third and fourth wings for stability, and a rudder was attached to the lower and second wing at the rear. A 9ft (2.7m) diameter propeller was fitted to the second wing from

The Vedovilli may have been the ugliest design of all time, though it would have a close competitor in another French design, the Dorand, which also was a total failure. The Vedovilli design makes it difficult to tell the front from the rear. In this photo the plane is facing forward. Bowers Collection

the bottom, tractor style. Skids were placed under each bottom wing tip.

No one at the old Cicero, Illinois, Flying Field ever remembers seeing the quadruplane's engine even run up.

Gary's Hoople Multiplane

William Pierce "Bing" Gary, of Washington, New Jersey, became interested in aviation in about 1905 when he designed a series of aircraft called Hooples, so called because each had a large, circular wing. The first design was actually a circular wing with a long tail boom resembling a dart. What passed for the fuselage was a pair of triangular tubes, and the engine was mounted at the apex of the triangles. It rested on a four-wheeled rectangle. Gary later modified the landing gear, moved the engine lower, and moved the pilot's position aft.

Gary's second model followed his basic design, except that he first tried opening the circular wing and forming a sort of wing panel by moving part of the wing downward, probably for better stability. Next, he made the same modification again but this time left the short wing in place and moved another section of the circular wing upward, thus creating two semicircular main sections plus a pair of stubby biplane wings. He succeeded in crashing this model. But, apparently he was able to salvage most of the plane for his final version of the Hoople.

For his final design Gary went back to the original circular wing, but this time he added three normal wings inside the circular wing struts, and a two-wheel landing gear with skids in front. He mounted the engine under the middle wing, and placed the "cockpit" directly below the engine. Gary retained the dart- or arrow-shaped tail and heavily rigged it with wire to add strength. He even built an odd-shaped hangar to house the Hoople.

There seems to have been three basic Hoople designs: one employing a concave hoop, one with a straight hoop, and a third with triplane wings. The amazing thing is that these Hooples actually flew, taking off from Union Avenue in Totowa, New Jersey. Gary later designed more conventional aircraft.

Girard Airship Multiplane

Henry Laurens Call invented the Girard Airship in 1908 at Girard, Kansas. It was a monster weighing 3,000lb (1,357.5kg) and powered by two 40hp motors driving four propellers, two tractor types in front and two pushers at the rear. A four-wheeled cart-like undercarriage supported the structure which, in some ways, resembled the Vedovilli creation.

The Airship's wings had a 2,300sq-ft (213.4sq-m) area. The middle wing was bent over the bottom portion and extended outward, and the top and bottom wings were mounted lengthwise to the fuselage. The rear of the fuselage resembled a lobster tail bent upward. At about 18ft (5.5m) high, to the local people the Girard must have been awe inspiring for its size as well as its complexity. Had it flown, they would have witnessed a real miracle!

Humphreys' Waterplane Tandem Multiplane

Jack Humphreys designed what may have been the first attempt at an amphibian. His waterplane was intended to be "capable of arising and alighting on both water and land." It was constructed at Wivenhoe, Essex, England, from 1908 to 1909.

Humphreys was known locally as "The Mad Dentist" and his machine was built around a kind of coracle hull made of very thin wood, in which the pilot sat. He must have had a fear of falling, though, since he stated that his design was geared toward eliminating practically all the dangers surrounding land flights in experimental machines: A fall from a considerable height need have no terrors with water below. It also would eliminate any possible hazards such as hedges, telegraph poles and wires, trees, ditches, fences, and so on. Humphreys also believed it possible to skid on water, while on land a skid would break the running gear or prove unresponsive to side influences.

Humphreys' multiplane contraption almost defies description. The hull had outrigger wing-tip floats and three wings above the hull. An engine was mounted in the middle wing, powering twin pusher propellers. Dozens of upright struts attached to the hull, and outriggers supported the wings and engine. The entire superstructure appeared top heavy, so it is doubtful that it was ever flown.

Jeansson and Colltex Tandem Hyproplane

Jeansson and Colltex designed and built a tandem-wing biplane hydroplane for the monarchy of Monaco in 1913. It had a wingspan of 79ft (24.1m), a length of 52ft (15.9m), and it stood 23ft (7.0m) high. The designers used a Despujols-type hull. Flying weight was 9,503lb (4,300kg). A pair of six-cylinder 230hp Chenu motors gave the multiplane a top speed of 62mph (100km/h).

Kaiser Multiplane

Chicago native Donald Kaiser designed and built his multiplane in 1912. He later became an air-mail pilot.

Kaiser's creation was a double biplane with a pair of wings forward and aft. The rear set of wings had cloth panels for added stability. The multiplane had a pair of wheels under the center fuselage and another pair under the rear wings; the latter were set close together. A maze of struts, rigging wires, and other bracings held the plane together. The fuselage appears to have been metal covered. The cockpit area strongly resembled that of a racing car of the period.

Apparently, the Kaiser never was successfully flown.

Ludlow Multiplane

Built by ten US Army soldiers in the Aeronautical Building at Jamestown, Ohio, the Ludlow multiplane made its public debut at the Jamestown Exposition being towed down the Miami River by a torpedo boat. During the course of the demonstration, the craft was wrecked. The engines had never been installed.

The designer, Israel Ludlow, had built a series of gliders that had proven successful. This aeromarine craft was a multiplane on floats and was constructed from water boilers, an old gasoline engine, strips of wood, and sheet iron with water planes (floats) of copper. Its four wings were unique in that the front and rear wings were large triangles, while the middle two wings were V-shaped. A pair of vertical planes were set in front. The pilot rode amidship, and the fuselage was raised above the floats by a maze of struts. It sloped from front to rear, with the front extremely high and the tail almost under water.

McCurd Multiplane

Little information seems to have survived about this aircraft, which is reported to have been under construction at North Finchley in the United Kingdom in 1909. It was to have had its wings adapted to be set at different angles of inclination. One half was coupled to the other half so as to move in an opposite direction.

Merx Fundecker Multiplane

This five-winged plane was reported to have been test flown at Flugplatz, Johannisthal, near Berlin, but it never left the ground. The multiplane had twin propellers and a four-wheel landing gear, plus a pair of front wheels attached to the struts. The wings were staggered from low in front to high in the rear. It resembled a wagon bed, with two-by-fours used for struts. The pulley-belt-operated propellers resembled windmill vanes and were mounted as pusher types. The entire craft looked a bit like the mobile stairways the airlines formerly used to debark passengers.

Phillips Multiplane

Horatio F. Phillips experimented with the theory of lifting surfaces from 1884 to 1891, and registered patents on six double-surface airfoils of varying gradation and camber that were intended to be used for aircraft wings. He formulated the theory that increased camber on the top of a double-surfaced wing creates a suction or reduced pressure above, thus providing lift. Later, he refined the shape of his double-surface airfoils to flatten the part of the leading edge into a biconvex shape to diminish drag and increase lift. He went on to build both models and full-size aircraft based on the idea that superimposed airfoils of his design, constructed with a high aspect ratio (long and narrow), would provide excellent lift.

In 1893, Phillips built his first of several multiplanes. The first had forty airfoils 19ft 1.5in (5.8m) long, set vertically behind a 6.5ft (2.0m) tractor propeller in a wheeled frame set on a circular track over 100yd (92.3m) in circumference. While he called it the Phillips I, it soon became known as the "Venetian Blind," for it resembled one. During testing, the rear wheel of the tricycle dolly lifted off the ground at 40mph (64.4km/h) but the rest remained firmly on the ground. A later model on a 200ft (61.0m) circuit lifted almost 400lb (181.0kg).

In 1904, Phillips installed a light gasoline engine in a twenty-camber airfoil design. This provided room enough for a pilot, and made the aircraft independent of any track. Though the lift was good, balance was incorrect and stability on the longitudinal axis was poor.

In 1907, using four banks of forty-eight airfoils in tandem behind a 7ft (2.1m) propeller driven by a 20hp engine, the Phillips multiplane lifted off the ground at Streamhan Common for 500ft (152.4m), making it the first powered flight in the United Kingdom—if the report was true.

Ravaud's Multiplane

Designed and built in 1908 by Roger Ravaud for the airplane and motorboat meets in Monaco, the Aeroscape was piloted by the designer in the 1909 Monaco contests. He never managed to get it off the water, however, and eventually it was destroyed in a crash.

The Aeroscape was one of the most unusual aircraft ever built. It was powered by a seven-cylinder Gnome engine with two concentric propellers mounted as pushers at the rear. No record mentions whether the two propellers that were mounted on the same shaft were contrarotating or not. The pilot sat in a small seat and steered by means of a motor car steering wheel. The three wings mounted not in the normal manner but above and parallel to the fuselage, giving next to no lift. The multiplane had a wheeled undercarriage, but apparently no control surfaces of any sort.

Roshon Multiplane

Built by an American named Roshon in 1908, in some respects, the multiplane resembled the Phillips "Venetian Blind." However, the Roshon was a double-tiered, box-like lattice-work structure which seems to have had three main wings, one in both the bottom and the center of the larger box, and a third at the top of the smaller box. The larger bottom box also had five regular-type wings mounted at the front while the smaller top box had five narrow wings at the front as well. Each box had another five wings mounted at its rear.

A four-wheel cart-like undercarriage of bicycle wheels provided for rolling takeoffs. A large, two-bladed propeller was attached tractor style. The three triplane wings that ran the entire length and width of the boxes were not flat, but were scalloped to make them concave. The frame was wooden, with metal tubing for struts, and cloth covered.

The Roshon seems sturdy enough to have at least lifted off the ground if the engine had sufficient power to get it rolling, but once airborne, control would have been a major problem.

Zerbe Multiplane

Professor J. S. Zerbe, of Compton, California, designed and built a five-wing multiplane to take part in the First Western Air Meet at Dominiques Field in 1910. The plane's five wings were staggered to the front and looked a bit like a stairway. A tricycle landing gear with one wheel in the rear and a rudder in front gave it a top-heavy look.

Running from January 10 through January 20, the meet attracted 100,000 spectators on a single day. Unfortunately, Zerbe never was able to get the plane off the ground.

Chapter 3

World War I Single-Seat Triplanes

The World War I era, from August 1914 to November 1918, saw the most rapid advance in airplane development of any period before or since. Military requirements dictated configuration, and some safety features such as tricycle landing gear vanished from the scene for many years.

The age of specialized airplanes emerged early in the war with the development of the fast single-seat scout. The scout was basically a product of the immediate prewar racing and speed-record-setting airplanes, the French Nieuport and Deperdussin monoplanes and the British Sopwith Tabloid biplane that won the 1914 Schneider Trophy Race.

While scouting behind enemy lines was the single-seater's primary mission, it was short-lived; the task was turned over to two-seater aircraft that carried the pilot and a trained observer. The name scout stuck, however, and some single-seaters were still called that by the popular press as late as 1918.

Late in 1915 the Dutch designer and builder Anthony H.G. "Tony" Fokker, working in Germany, developed a synchronized machine-gun installation that allowed the guns to fire through the propeller arc and permitted the pilot to aim the guns by pointing the plane's nose at the enemy. Thus, the single-seater achieved its major role. Now its purpose was to seek out and destroy enemy aircraft, primarily the two-seater observation planes. History is full of fact and fiction accounts of "dogfights" between large groups of opposing single-seaters. While such actions did take place, that was not the real job of the single-seater. Its mission now was to prevent bombers from reaching their target, and to make sure that enemy observation planes didn't see what was going on behind the lines.

The French called their single-seaters *Chasseurs*, which translates to "Pursuit" in English, and was the term used officially by the Americans. Other nations called them "fighters." Some were kept on standby to defend specific targets and were called "alerts."

The first effective triplane fighter was the British Sopwith of late 1916, actually an adaptation of the Sopwith Pup biplane that was a direct development of the prewar Tabloid. The Sopwith Tripehound, an unofficial name for the triplane, made a great impression on the Germans. After capturing a few examples, they invited the German aircraft industry to examine

them with the idea of developing an equivalent or superior type as quickly as possible. The period from mid-1917 to early 1918 saw the greatest number of triplane developments in history.

Many of the wartime triplane designs on both sides followed the Sopwith example of simply adding an extra wing to a proven biplane design, thus greatly reducing the lead time to produce a new airplane. Very few World War I triplane fighters were designed from scratch.

While the new German triplanes were inspired by Sopwith, a number of Allied designers produced triplanes with little, if any, knowledge of the Sopwith triplane. The triplane was pretty well obsolete by late 1918, but some designs then under development were not completed until the following year. These designs are included in this chapter, but some with notable postwar careers are also covered in chapter 6.

AEG Triplanes

The Allgemeine Elektrizitats Gesellschaft, abbreviated to AEG for general reference, was a large German electrical firm, similar to the American General Electric Company. AEG had formed an aircraft division before the start of World War I. Its principal wartime products were observation types and twin-engine bombers, but it also tried its hand at producing triplanes: two single-seat fighters and a two-seat observation plane.

Dr.I

The AEG Dr.I was a quick adaptation of a limited-production-run AEG D.I biplane which had been introduced in May of 1917. Its distinguishing feature was its slightly elliptical wings connected by single I-struts. The Dr.I was powered by a standard 160hp Mercedes D.III engine. The fuselage was unusually deep for a single-seat plane of that era, leading us (the authors) to believe that the airplane used a shortened fuselage and other parts of the contemporary AEG C.VIII two-seat airplane.

The Dr.I structure was unusual by contemporary German designs, as it used a welded-steel fuselage, tail, and wing spars with wooden ribs. The D.Is deep fuselage made it easy to convert to a triplane type, in November of 1917. The center wing was attached to the fuselage just below the upper longerons. Strut-con-

The AEG Dr.I was adapted from the D.I biplane simply by substituting triplane wings. The plane featured a bulky, side-mounted radiator—thoroughly obsolete for fighters by late 1917. Bowers Collection

nected ailerons were used on the upper and lower wings only. The Dr.I triplane version was unusual in that it had a greater wingspan than its biplane predecessor. It proved to be no more maneuverable than the D.I, but was nearly 20mph (32.2km/h) slower and so was not developed further.

Specifications:
Span 30ft 10¹/₈in (7.7m); length 20ft ¹/₄in (6.1m); empty weight 1,582lb (715.8kg); gross weight 2,134lb (965.6kg); top speed 106.25mph (171.1km/h).

PE
The PE was an early 1918 effort at an armored single-seat ground-attack plane. Apparently, it carried only an unofficial company designation of PE for Panzer Einsitzer (armored single-seater). PE does not fit into any known list of official designations, in which J stands for armored.

The PE's metal-framed fuselage was covered with smooth sheet aluminum, and the engine and cockpit areas were armored. The engine was a new and untried Benz Bz IIIb, a notable departure from German practice in being a V-8 type.

The triplane's wings were inspired by the Dr.I with the steel-tube spars and two bays of I-struts. As on the Dr.I, strut-connected ailerons were on the upper and lower wings only. Armament consisted of two forward-firing Spandau LGM 08/15 machine guns and four light bombs.

The PE proved to be an interesting deviation from the practice of converting existing biplane designs to triplanes. It was designed from the start as a triplane, but failing in that configuration, it was redeveloped as a biplane using the same fuselage, empennage, and engine and designated the DJ.I. The DJ.I, combining the D nomenclature in which D stood for single-seat fighter and J for armored airplane, appeared in September of 1918.

Specifications:
Span 36.75ft (11.2m); length 21ft 7⁷/₈in (6.6m); empty weight 2,600lb (1,176.5kg); gross weight 3,106lb (1,405.4kg); top speed 103.5mph (166.6km/h); rate of climb to 3,280ft (1,000m) 5.8min.

The AEG PE was designed as an armored triplane for ground-attack missions but was developed further as a biplane, the DJ.I. Heinz J. Nowarra Collection

The first Albatros triplane was a standard D.Va model that had been converted simply by fitting triplane wings. As with the production D.Vs, the Dr.I had the unpainted plywood fuselage but used the standard printed-lozenge camouflage pattern cloth on the fabric surfaces. Bowers Collection

Albatros Triplanes

The Albatros Werke GmbH at Johannisthal, a suburb of Berlin, had been designing and manufacturing aircraft since 1910, so when their designer Robert

No mistaking the Albatros D.II; it carried the designation on its fuselage. All components except the wings were from the D.X fighter. The wings had a more efficient arrangement than those of the Dr.I. Bowers Collection

Thelen turned to designing fighters, he produced an outstanding line culminating in the Albatros D.V and D.Va. In time, however, their performances had been equaled or surpassed by newer Allied planes, including the Sopwith triplane. So he sought a quick fix by fitting three wings to a standard D.V, resulting in the Dr.I triplane. The new machine was test flown in July of 1917.

The triplane wings, while similar to the lower wing of the D.V in both dimension and shape, were built up around two spars to avoid the problems encountered with the lower wing under load conditions. The weight caused the wing to flex enough to break away from the wing strut, which led to a complete failure of the wing structure. The upper and lower wings were built in one piece while the middle wing was split into two halves. The upper wing had a decreased chord and was mounted above the fuselage on N-type center section struts. The middle wing halves were attached to the fuselage slightly above the longitudinal centerline and had a cutout to improve the pilot's downward view. The lower wing had a similar cutout, and the bottom wing was suspended below the fuselage by small struts. The cutout on the bottom wing also provided room to attach the rear undercarriage struts. Interplane struts and bracing wires connected each set of wings. Ailerons were attached to each set of wings and connected on each side by rods,

Placement of the two core-type radiators for the 185hp Benz engine was not only odd, but was very inefficient by 1918 standards. Heinz J. Nowarra Collection

with the operating cables being channeled through the center wing to the fuselage.

In spite of Thelen's efforts the performance of the Dr.I was unimpressive, and he fell from grace with the German Air Force.

Specifications:

Powerplant, 160hp Mercedes; span 15 ft 8in (7.1m); length 24ft (7.3m); top speed 132mph (212.5km/h).

Austin Motor Company Triplane

The British Austin Motor Company, having established an aviation department during the war, decided to compete with the Sopwith Snipe in a private venture by designing a triplane they hoped would be able to equal or better the Snipe's performance. Their designer, C. H. Brooks, came up with a design that, in many ways, resembled the Sopwith Tripehound.

Named the Osprey, the plane featured wooden construction with fabric covering. It was powered by a 230hp Bentley nine-cylinder rotary B.R.2 engine. Test flown for the first time in February of 1918, the Osprey proved to be inferior in performance to the Snipe, so construction halted on the second and third prototypes. The company attempted to develop other experimental aircraft, but none were successful.

The Osprey's armament was unique in that while the plane had a normal arrangement of fixed forward-firing synchronized twin .303cal Vickers machine guns, it also had a single semi-free .303cal Lewis gun on the rear spanwise member of the middle-wing center section. Care probably had to be taken when using it so as not to hit a part of the aircraft.

Specifications:

Span 23ft (7.0m); length 17ft 7in (5.4m); height 10ft 8in (3.3m); wing area 233sq-ft (21.6sq-m); empty weight 1,106lb (500.5kg); gross weight 1,888lb (854.3kg); maximum speed 118mph (190.0km/h) at 10,000ft (3,048.8m); rate of climb to 10,000ft 10 minutes

Photos showing fully assembled but uncovered triplanes such as this are on the rare side. The solid-wood-center wing spar is routed out for lightness while the top and bottom wing spars are built-up box construction. William Green Collection

37

20 seconds; endurance three hours. Austin had assigned the model designation of A.F.T.3, for Austin Fighter Triplane.

Berg Triplane

This is one aircraft whose name can be confusing at times. The manufacturing company was the Aviatik GmbH Osterreischiche-ungarish Flugzeugfabrik,

Profile illustrating the lightness and balance of the Osprey. Visible are its rectangular rudder, heavy tail skid, and the

Austin Motor Company logo on the nose behind the cowl. Bowers Collection

This three-quarter front view of the Osprey shows the strut arrangements and the rigging wires, as well as the engine and twin Vickers machine-gun mountings. Bowers Collection

With the plane sitting on the turf, you can see the gaps between the center wing and the fuselage. The fabric on the fuselage side sags. Imperial War Museum, London

Wien (Vienna), the Austrian affiliate of the German Automobil und Aviatikwerke AG. But since the designer was Dipl. Ing. Julius von Berg, it bears his name even though some sources state that Prof. Richard Knoller had a hand in the design work.

The Dr.I triplane was a direct adaptation of the Berg D.I of late 1917 and early 1918. The Aviatik D.I has been considered the best all-Austrian fighter of the war. It had a good rate of speed and an excellent rate of climb, but its Austro-Daimler engine had a long-standing problem overheating. The lower wing was placed below the fuselage on the triplane to keep the center of drag as close as possible to the old, and to make certain there was a minimum of change in flight characteristics and trim between the two- and three-wing versions. Basically, the design simply came too late in the war to be pursued.

The Berg's powerplant was a 200hp Austro-Daimler. Wingspan reached 23ft (7.0m), and the plane was 22ft 9½in long (6.9m), had 242sq-ft (22.5sq-m) of wing area, and weighed 1,900lb (859.7kg) gross. Wing stagger was a mere 7in (17.8cm), with a chord of 4.75ft (1.5m). A four-bladed propeller replaced the 9ft (2.7m) two-bladed type of the standard D.I.

Bezobrazov Triplane

This 1917 Russian triplane single-seater was designed by Ens. A. A. Bezobrazov and can either be classified as a tailless aircraft with an extremely high degree of wing stagger (approximately 60deg), or as a triple tandem monoplane. Because of the conventional fuselage and the presence of a vertical fin and rudder, we believe it belongs in the triplane classification.

With no horizontal tail, the elevators on the Bezobrazov were located in the center of the lower wing. Longitudinal stability was provided by the great separation of the top and bottom wings, using the characteristics of a tandem-wing design. Ailerons were fitted to the two upper wings. A pylon on the fuselage above the center wing supported the landing wires to the lower wing, while the strutless center section of the upper wing, located far ahead of the 80hp Gnome rotary engine, was supported by the interplane struts through a system of kingposts and wires.

The Austrian affiliate of the German Automobil und Aviatikwerke, AG, known as Aviatik, built aircraft popularly known as Berg. The Dr.I was another of those "instant" triplanes created by adding a third wing. It is shown next to the Berg D.I from which it was created. J. M. Bruce Collection

Profile of the Dr.I shows the dappled form of camouflage used on the airplane. The German Iron Cross can be seen on the wheel cover and rudder. Heinz J. Nowarra Collection

Side view of the Russian Bezobrazov triplane shows the extreme stagger of the three wings. In the absence of a horizontal tail these provide longitudinal stability, as though

the plane were a tandem-wing instead of a rather freakish triplane. Heinz J. Nowarra Collection

It should be noted that the triplane's wings had the highest aspect ratio—span divided by chord—of any airplane built up to that time. Unfortunately, the Bezobrazov is reported to have crashed on its first flight.

The only known photo of the Blackburn triplane reveals a number of design features: the Clerget 110hp rotary engine, mounted pusher style; the twin vertical tail surfaces, mounted on twin booms; the cockpit nacelle; and the forward-staggered wings. J. M. Bruce Collection

Specifications:

Span 57ft 8in (17.6m); length 27.25ft (8.3m); wing area 283sq-ft (26.3sq-m); empty weight 880lb (398.2kg); gross weight 1,210lb (547.5kg).

Blackburn Triplane

Robert Blackburn was a civil engineer working for an engineering consultants firm in Rouen, France, in 1908 when he witnessed Wilbur Wright flying at Issy and decided to get involved in aeronautics. He designed a number of monoplanes and biplanes that enjoyed some success, and formed the Blackburn Aeroplane Company in Yorkshire, England, where he was still manufacturing sport airplanes when World War I commenced.

In 1915 Blackburn's firm developed a single-seat fighter triplane to provide unrestricted forward firepower, in the days before the synchronized machine gun was developed. To provide more power, the original 100hp Gnome rotary was replaced by a 110hp Clerget. Blackburn's more or less radical design was passed over in favor of more conservative types and the proposed fighter was quickly forgotten. British records on the triplane are so sparse that it is not known if the prototype was the only one manufactured.

Breda-Pensuti Triplane

Italian Emilio Pensuti developed the Messenger in an effort to design the smallest aircraft possible to be

The small size of the Pensuti is obvious in relation to the men in this photo. Downward vision of the pilot had to be limited by the center wing. Courtesy F. Gordon Swanborough

sort of an aerial version of a motorcycle. The prototype was built at the Caproni factory and thus was known as the Caproni-Pensuti. After Pensuti died in a vain rescue attempt, Breda took over the design and produced at least one improved version. At the end of the war, no further attempt was made to produce the design because of the uncertainty of postwar avaiation in Italy.

Specifications:

Powerplant, Anzani six-cylinder 40hp radial; span 13ft 1½in (4.0m); length 14ft 4.75in (4.4m); gross weight 638lb (288.7kg); top speed 80mph (128.8km/h).

Curtiss Triplanes

In 1915 Glenn Curtiss moved his aircraft factory from Hammondsport to Buffalo, New York, about one hundred miles northwest, but engine production remained at Hammondsport. Until the United States entered the war in April of 1917, Curtiss airplane production in Buffalo was scattered among several plants around town. By that July, however, the US government had centralized the Curtiss facilities under one roof—the seventy-two-acre North Elmwood Plant which the government built for Curtiss. After that, most of Curtiss' aeronautical development activities were overseen by one management company: the new Curtiss Aeroplane and Motor Company.

Up to 1917, Curtiss had been producing mostly twin-engine flying boats for Great Britain and the US Navy, and two-seat biplane trainers. In addition, they built and tested a few experimental civilian models until civil flying was shut down in 1917 to concentrate on the war effort.

From 1916 through 1918, Curtiss turned out some fifteen separately designated triplane designs. These were enough to make the company the world's most prolific triplane designer, even though few attained production status. Of the fifteen triplanes designed, five were single-seaters and are presented here.

S-1

S-series triplane construction began early in 1916 when Curtiss built the S-1, the smallest biplane that could carry the 90–100hp Curtiss OX-series engine. Although the S-1 was a single-seater, the letter S did not stand for scout, it was simply an alphabetical sequence of Curtiss model designations.

S-2

Since the wing area of the S-1 was inadequate, the wings were enlarged, thus producing the S-2. The second S-series biplane had a similar airframe, but the wings were braced with struts to test a "wireless" type construction. Neither the S-1 nor the S-2 were ever put into production.

S-3

The S-3 was the true triplane version of the S-1 and S-2, with a span of 25ft (7.6m), length of 19ft 6in (6.0m), and a 100hp Curtiss OXX-2 engine. It reached a top speed of 115mph (185.2km/h), making it the fastest American airplane when it flew in September of 1916. This performance impressed the Army, which ordered four improved versions later in the year, assigning Army serial numbers 322–325 to the project. Machine-gun armament was specified but never installed, and of course, no S-3s were sent overseas after the United States entered the war. All that the S-3 accomplished was to point out how far the United States had lagged

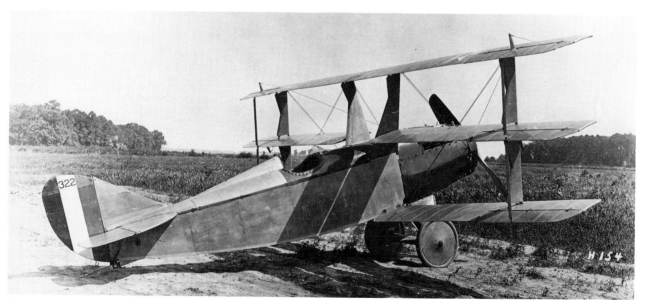

The Curtiss S-3 was the first single-seat Scout ordered by the US Army. Note the K-shaped struts. The star-in-circle insignia for wings and stripes for the rudder were adopted *for US military airplanes after the United States entered the war. Signal Corps via the National Archives*

behind Europe in the development of high-performance airplanes. Curtiss had been able to compete with its big flying boats and low-powered trainers, but the US government and aircraft industry were completely isolated from the rapid European military developments.

The Curtiss S-4 and S-5 triplanes were identical airframes differing only in that the S-4 was fitted with twin floats and the S-5 with a single main float. Wingspan, as shown here during land-plane tests, was increased over that of the S-3 to compensate for the weight of the floats. Dustin Carter Collection

Specifications:

Powerplant, Curtiss OXX-2; span 25ft (7.6m); length 19.5ft (6.0m); wing area 142.6sq-ft (13.2sq-m); gross weight 1,320lb (597.3kg); maximum speed 112mph (180.32km/h).

S-4

The S-4 was a triplane similar to the S-3, and ordered by the US Navy which assigned it Navy Bu. No. A-149. As a seaplane it was Curtiss' first experience with twin floats on a Scout. As with other Curtiss seaplanes, it became necessary to increase the wingspan to compensate for the weight of the floats. After delivery to the Navy, the forward float struts collapsed during a hard landing in January of 1918, and the plane was scrapped.

The S-5, a sister ship of the S-4, and assigned Navy Bu. No. A-150, differed in having only a single main float and wing-tip floats. It survived until August of 1919.

S-6

The S-6 was a slightly enlarged version of the S-3, and the US Army ordered twelve S-6's early in 1917. However, only Army serial number 492 was actually delivered. The S-6 was the first American Scout fitted with machine guns, but these may have been mounted only for demonstration purposes or for show. They

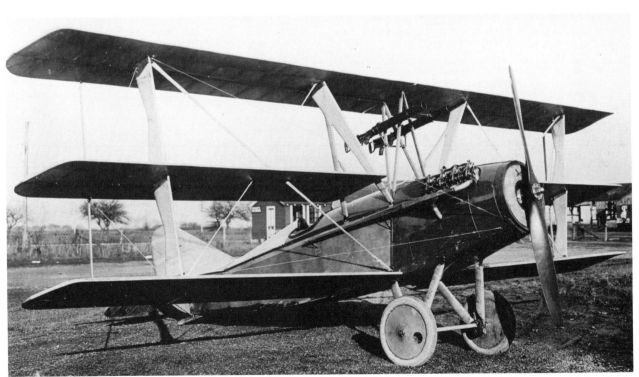

The single Curtiss S-6 was a slightly enlarged and refined S-3 intended to be armed with two machine guns. The position of the drum-fed Lewis guns made it impossible for the pilot to *reload in flight. The guns may have been added only for propaganda purposes. Bowers Collection*

were gas-operated Lewis guns, unsuited for synchronized fire through the propeller, and their positioning high and ahead of the pilot made it impossible to change the drums while in flight. Nothing is known of the service history of the S-6.

GS-1

The GS-1 was the result of a US Navy contract calling for five single-seat biplane seaplanes (still called Scouts) to be powered with the 100hp French Gnome rotary engine. The surprisingly logical designation of GS for Gnome Scout was assigned to the project. Incidentally, this was the first and *only* Curtiss airplane to be designed for a rotary engine. The designation was changed to GS-1 and GS-2 when a sixth airframe was added to the contract.

Although this was the sixth airplane, it was the first one completed and therefore became the GS-1. It differed from its followers in being a triplane instead of a biplane as ordered. The GS-1 had very narrow wings with a wide gap to give an efficient gap-to-chord ratio. An odd feature was the use of shock absorbers between the main float and the fuselage. This resulted in near-disastrous porpoising due to the changing angle between the float and the fuselage during high-speed runs. The GS-1, assigned Bu. No. A-868, was delivered to the Navy on January 1, 1918. It had a very short operational life, however; a Navy pilot crashed it during a landing just three months later.

DFW Triplane

The Deutsche Flugzeugwerke (DFW) was an old established firm before World War I that produced the Taube monoplane. When the war broke out DFW turned to producing training planes and large observation planes. Then in 1917 it began designing a fighter airplane, developing a basic model—the Dr.I—that could serve as either a biplane or a triplane.

The design called for a laminated wood veneer fuselage, which was a radical departure from standard company practice of using slab-sided plywood structures. The Dr.I had staggered wings, and the bottom wing was set below the fuselage on struts. The wing tip on the top wing was rounded, while the other wing tips were more angular. Twin sets of N-struts were used on each wing, joining top, center, and bottom wings.

The Dr.I had an experimental 180hp Korting six-cylinder inline engine installed, replacing the 160hp Mercedes used initially. The biplane version used a 150hp Benz engine.

The DFW triplane was eliminated from fighter competition in 1918, and dropped from production.

Euler Triplanes

German pioneer aviator and manufacturer August Euler continued building airplanes during the war in his small plant in Frankfurt-am-Main where, in association with the Austro-Hungarian designer Julius Hromadnik, he turned out a great number of experimental designs. Euler concentrated on producing training biplanes and the designs of others, including 100 copies of the French Nieuport 11 fighters that the German Army had asked industry to develop from captured specimens. This experience encouraged Hromadnik to develop several other fighters of his own design, some of which obviously had been inspired by the Nieuport.

Among the Euler experimentals were four single-seat fighter triplanes. None of these were purchased by the Flugzeugmeisterei (Aircraft Master Office) for the

The US Navy Curtiss GS-1 delivered in January of 1918 had the distinction of being the only Curtiss airplane designed to use a rotary engine. Paul Matt Collection

The Deutsche Flugzeugwerke AG (DFW) Dr.I, a stagger-wing triplane fighter, was entered in the 1918 fighter competition at Adlershof. Powered by a Mercedes 160hp inline water-cooled engine, it was derived from the D.I. Initially, the Dr.I was powered by the 170hp Korting six-cylinder inline experimental engine. The top wing had a rounded tip, the middle wing was square tipped, and the bottom wing tip was curved slightly. The fuselage was laminated wood veneer. The plane was eliminated from the competition and did not go into production. Bowers Collection

Luftstreitkrafte (German Air Force), so they never received an official designation. However, aero-historians have identified them in approximately their chronological order, with the standard Dr (triplane) designations. Details and designations follow:

Triplane Type II (also referred to as Dr.I): Although the first of the Euler single-seat triplane fighters, this model is referred to as Type II because it followed an earlier and larger Euler military triplane design. Powered with the twin-row fourteen-cylinder Oberursel Ur.III rotary engine, a license-built copy of the 160hp French Gnome, the Type II drew heavily on Nieuport detail and incorporated a unique wing and strut arrangement that featured a two-spar upper wing and single-spar middle and lower wings in the Nieuport style. This arrangement obviously inspired the later Pfalz Dr.I.

Triplane Type III (also referred to as Dr.II): Type III was a late 1917 design fitted with the then-standard German fighter engine, the 160hp Mercedes D.III. The single-spar wings had an exceptionally narrow chord, apparently in hope of overcoming the drag of three wings by increasing their efficiency through an increased gap-to-chord ratio. The design was unsuccessful and in a departure from the practice of the day, was rebuilt as a biplane.

Triplane Type IV (also referred to as Dr.III): The third variant was the Euler triplane that came closest to achieving success. It was powered by a new Goebel Goe.III rotary engine. Although not of the cantilever design, Type IV's wings owed more to Fokker than to Nieuport. It was capable of reaching an altitude of 16,405ft (5,000m) in 13.5 minutes, a good performance at the time. The Type IV was entered in the German Fighter Competition in May 1918, but failed to win an order. The tail was damaged in a taxiing accident and the plane was sent back to the factory.

Triplane Type V (also referred to as Dr.IV): The final Euler triplane started as an adaptation of the so-called quadruplane fighter in that the upper wing was removed and the other three wings were retained in their original positions. The wings were soon rearranged to increase the gap, however, and the unconventional idea of pivoting the upper wing to serve as ailerons was tried again on the Type V triplane. The Type V was then fitted with a 110hp Siemens-Halske

The first Euler single-seat triplane was the Type II, with a 160hp Oberursel Ur.III engine and a two-spar upper wing, but single-spar center and lower wings. Heinz J. Nowarra Collection

The Euler Type III used the 160hp Mercedes water-cooled engine and featured very narrow single-spar wings. The radiator was built into the center section of the upper wing. Joseph Nieto Collection

The Euler Type IV featured a fuselage, landing gear, and engine cowl much like that of the French Nieuport II fitted

with triplane wings that fitted neatly to the fuselage, as on the later Fokker triplane. Peter M. Grosz Collection

Sh.I engine. The upper wing-cum-aileron system proved to be unsuccessful, so the wing was then fixed in place and standard ailerons were installed.

Fokker Triplanes

Most famous of all World War I triplanes, even more so than the British Sopwith that inspired it, was the German Fokker Dr.I. Dr was the German designation for *Dreidecker* or triplane. The Fokker Dr.I, with some 330 built, was the most produced triplane of all time. It was an excellent two-gun fighter, albeit a little slow and underpowered for its time. But its accomplishments have been exaggerated in later years, partially due to the charisma of Manfred von Richthofen, "The Red Baron," who scored nineteen of his eighty victories while flying the triplane. He also was killed while flying one.

While other manufacturers, notably Curtiss, Euler, and Sopwith, developed a greater number of separate triplane designs, the variously numbered Fokkers are a prime example of the evolutionary development of a single basic design. As such, they are worthy of a more detailed presentation than the others.

The Dutch designer Anthony H.G. "Tony" Fokker, unable to obtain flight instruction in his own country, took his training in Germany in 1910. He got his pilot's certificate on May 16, 1911. Fokker and Oberleutnant Franz von Daum formed a partnership of sorts and built several aircraft, but Fokker soon became associated with boat builder Jacob Goedecker at Nieder-Walluf. Together they turned out an improved model Spin using Fokker's plans. Next Fokker moved his operation to Johannisthal, a suburb of

Berlin. In October of 1913, the nomadic Fokker moved his factory and part of his successful flying school to Gorries, near Schwerin, in the northern German province of Mecklenburg, where it remained until several years after the end of World War I.

It was here that Fokker—asked by the German Air Force to examine and improve on Roland Garros' device for firing a machine gun through the propeller arc—perfected a superior system to the French ace's bullet deflector idea—a true synchronizer that made the single-seater a deadly fighting machine. The age of the famous aces began after the Fokker synchronizer was installed on the Fokker M.5 (E-1) Eindecker in mid-1915. The success of this and later Fokker E-types originated the legend that the defenseless British reconnaissance planes were just "Fokker Fodder."

Early in 1917 Fokker, along with other German designers, was invited by the Air Force to inspect a captured British Sopwith triplane with the idea of producing an equal or preferably better German triplane fighter. This official encouragement was just what Fokker needed; his star had faded as other more modern designs replaced his Eindeckers, which were basically prewar designs.

Fokker already had a head start with some new design concepts. As a result of an officially forced association with Prof. Hugo Junkers—the advocate of the all-metal cantilever-winged monoplanes—Fokker had been sold on the merits of thick-section cantilever wings, ones that eliminated the traditional arrangement of struts and wires.

Fokker and his chief designer produced the V.1, a novel sesquiplane. The V designation originally stood for *Verspannungslos*, the German word meaning a

The Euler Type V triplane, after the pivoted upper wing that doubled as the ailerons was rebuilt as a fixed flying surface with separate inset conventional ailerons. Heinz J. Nowarra Collection

wing without bracing (cantilever). Later it came to mean *Versuchs,* or experimental.

The Floh (flea) V.1, powered by a 100hp Oberursel rotary engine, was underpowered for a fighter even by early 1917 standards. For maximum streamlining, the rectangular steel-tubing fuselage frame was rounded out by wooden formers and stringers to fair with the round engine cowling. The wings, with two wooden box spars, were covered with plywood for torsional stiffness. Similar V.2 and V.3 models were also built but were fitted with 120hp inline six water-cooled Mercedes engines. It is possible that the low power can be explained by assuming that the V.1 through V.3 models were simply proof-of-concept prototypes, not fighter prototypes as such.

(*Note:* In this presentation of Fokker triplanes, the airplanes are in sequence of design development, rather than being grouped by designation. First, there are the V-models that led to the production F.I and Dr.I; then on to the later V-models derived from the Dr.I. The V.3 was a triplane. Also note that for many years, the V.4 prototype has been misidentified as the V.3 in Fokker histories. The recent identification of what had been thought of as a modified V.2 as the actual V.3 by historian Peter M. Grosz, corrected the erroneous designations of V.3 and V.4 for the Fokker prototypes to V.4 and V.5.)

V.4

For his new triplane, Fokker chief designer Rheinhold Platz greatly simplified the fuselage structure of the V.1 by reverting to a rectangular cross section with round cowling for the 110hp Oberursel Ur.III rotary engine. The change of cross sections was accommodated by a stringer and plywood fairing from the firewall to a point behind the cockpit. The comma-shaped rudder reverted to the older Fokker models, but a fixed horizontal stabilizer was new to Fokker practice via the V.3. The landing gear featured the

unique small wing section built around the cross axle as introduced on the V.1, and was to become a Fokker trademark on into the postwar years. The lift generated by this airfoil reportedly carried the weight of the landing gear.

The fuselage of the V.4 was proportionally deeper than that of the Sopwith, allowing the lower wing to be built into the bottom as on the Sopwith. The middle wing rested on top of the upper longerons where it faired neatly into the turtle deck, unlike that of the inefficient inner-end of the Sopwith middle wing which was well above the longerons.

The V.4's wings carried Fokker's new enthusiasm for *Verspannungslos* (cantilever) to an extreme. The two lower wings attached to the fuselage through four bolt-on fittings each, but the upper wing was supported only by two steel-tube inverted vees which formed the center section struts. There were no traditional struts connecting the wings, and of course no flying or landing wire rigging. Roll loads for the upper wing were taken only by a pair of crossed wires between the center section struts.

The three wings were fabric covered. In the absence of struts or plywood covering, torsional stiffness was obtained in a novel way. Each wing had two closely spaced box spars that were bridged top and bottom by plywood to produce a rigid structure. The plywood around the leading edges of the wings was for aerodynamic smoothness, not torsional stiffness. Bolting points on the tops of the center section struts attached to the top wing at the front and rear faces of the double box spar, and ensured rigidity of that wing in all axes relative to the fuselage. Unbalanced ailerons were fitted to the upper wing only, and the elevators were unbalanced as well.

After Fokker's own test flights, the V.4 was flown by German ace Werner Voss at the factory, where the flights were observed by German officials. Like most Fokker prototypes the V.4 flew without military mark-

The first Fokker triplane was the cantilever-wing V.4 which was notable for the absence of traditional interplane struts and flying wires. It was a silvery gray. Photographed at Schwerin, Germany, this plane has long been erroneously identified as the V.3. Robert C. Hare Collection

Three-quarter rear view of the V.4 shows the intersection of the center and bottom wings with the fuselage. Compare horizontal tail and upper wing-tip shapes to later Fokker triplane variants. Coen Smit Collection

ings, but crosses were soon applied. After being fitted with later V.5 wings and other improvements, the V.4 was purchased by the German Air Force under the F.1 contract and was sent by Fokker to Austria-Hungary as a demonstrator. However, no orders for production models were received from that source.

V.5

In contrast to assigning V-numbers to single prototypes, Fokker next built three improved versions of the V.4 as V.5s, constructor numbers 1697, 1729, and 1730. These had slightly more span to the upper and middle wings, horn-balanced ailerons and elevators, a slightly lengthened fuselage, and most notably, I-type struts between the wings. It is a part of the Fokker legend that these were added for psychological reasons—pilots simply would not trust wings without the traditional struts. Actually the struts did contribute to the overall rigidity of the wing system, both in bending and torsion.

The second and third V.5s were armed with two LMG 08/15 machine guns. Their performance and

The Fokker V.5, long misidentified as the V.4, added armament, revised wings with overhanging balanced ailerons on the upper, and balanced elevators to the basic V.4 design. It *was tested at the IdFleig in Adlershof.* Heinz J. Nowarra Collection

The three Fokker F.1 triplanes were pre-production versions of the V.5. Here Tony Fokker demonstrates F.1 serial number 102/17 to General von Lossberg, Manfred von Richthofen ("The Red Baron"), ace Kurt Wolff, and other officers. Later, von Richthofen scored two victories in this plane. Alex Imrie Collection

Ace Werner Voss and his Fokker F.1 103/17. Note the face painted on the engine cowling. Voss, flying alone, was boxed in by six British S.E.5s and shot down on September 23, 1918. Heinz J. Nowarra Collection

apparent strength impressed the officials to the point that they ordered twenty production models, with the prototypes to be included in the contract. Follow-on orders eventually resulted in a total of 320 Fokker triplane fighters.

F.I

The last three of the Fokker triplane prototypes received the official German Air Force designation of F.I, and were assigned a new block of military serials beginning with 101/17. Apparently the use of the F designation was an attempt to use a letter following A through E, which were then in use, to identify a new category—a triplane fighter as distinct from the D and E types. However, it was applied to only the last three Fokker prototypes.

The first of the four were sent to Austria-Hungary after being redesignated the Dr.I; the second was static tested as required by the German Air Force; and the last two were sent to Baron von Richthofen's fighter unit at Coutray, on the British front, for combat evaluation.

The German Air Force serial numbers were issued on an annual basis within designated types. By 1917 each number series started at 100, followed by a slash and the last two digits of the year. For example, F.I 100/17 was the first F-type contracted for in 1917. However, serial number 100/17 was not assigned until much later; the first F.I built was 101/17. The full range of serial numbers covered the Fokker F.I and Dr.I models 100/17 through 220/17 and 400/17 through 599/17. There was a rebuilt Dr.I that was re-serialed as 100/18. These add up to more than the recorded total of 330 delivered, so there must have been some cancellations of Fokkers or an assignment of serials to other manufacturers for Dr types that were not used.

Despite its low-power engine at the time, the Fokker triplane proved to be a thoroughly good fighter—light on the controls, extremely maneuverable, and able to hold altitude in tight turns. In describing it to his fellow pilots, Manfred von Richthofen said it "could climb like an ape and was as agile as the devil." It could outclimb many of its opponents, but one significant performance handicap was its relatively low speed; enemies could often escape it by simply outrunning it.

German ace Werner Voss scored a victory with F.I. 103/17 on his first operational flight in the machine on August 30, 1917. Over the next twenty days he reportedly scored ten additional victories in what must be considered the most spectacular and successful combat debut of any fighter. Voss, whose final score was forty-eight, was shot down by British pilot A.P.F. Rhys-Davis, one of a flight of six S.E.5's that boxed in Voss' lone Fokker on September 23.

Richthofen flew F.I 102/17 at the front on September 7 and scored his sixtieth victory, soon followed by a second kill. The Fokker's performance greatly impressed him and he urged that his J.G. 1 be equipped with it as soon as possible. Another ace, Kurt Wolff with thirty-three victories, was shot down in F.I 102/17 on September 15. Richthofen returned to flying Albatros D.Vs for a while, scoring two more victories with it before taking an extended leave in September. The brief but spectacular combat career of the two F.I. models was over.

Dr.I

The designation of the Fokker F.I was officially changed to Dr.I on August 16, 1917, but the assigned F.I serial numbers continued. Outwardly the only difference between the Dr.I and the F.I was the addition of wooden lower wing-tip skids to the Dr.I, and a more rearward location of the fuselage crosses.

As the only production-model German triplanes, the Fokker F.Is and Dr.Is carried standard German military markings and were subject to the changes that pertained to them. Fokker, neither a military man nor a German, was lax both in the matter of military markings and airplane camouflage on production models. He was the last to use the highly visible white squares on wings and fuselage as backgrounds for the curved-arm German Iron Crosses (called *Patee* or *Formee* in heraldry). Not until early 1918, partway into Fokker D.VII production, did he adopt the four- and five-color lozenge-pattern camouflage that was printed on the fabric before it was applied to the airplane. This had been in use by other manufacturers before the Fokker triplanes were built.

Fokker had a camouflage scheme exclusively his own. The top and side surfaces were covered with white fabric. He had these painted with a greenish-brown pigmented dope which was applied by brush, using an almost dry brush and thick dope in a way that the pigment did not cover the white well. This resulted in vertical streaks on the fuselage sides, and diagonal streaks on the wings, horizontal tail, and top of the fuselage—poor work from a meticulous painter's point of view, but very effective in creating a camouflage pattern. The undersurfaces were properly painted sky blue.

All the F.Is and Dr.Is were delivered with the white squares that were no longer in use by other manufacturers. In combat zones these were often eliminated, but not always by painting over the white areas—except for the standard 50mm white border for the Iron Cross. In March of 1918, it was directed that the curved-arm crosses be changed to a straight-arm type (a Greek cross), called the *Balkenkreuze* by the Germans. Some were still painted on white squares, while others received white borders to increase their visibility on a dark background.

By early 1918 the German Air Force allowed a departure from the camouflage as a morale builder. German *Jastas* were allowed to paint their planes in vivid individual color schemes. Earlier, each squadron had used single color or unit badge for identification. The wild colors led British pilots to call such squadrons "Flying Circuses," and the name stuck.

Production Fokker Dr.I 513/17 displays the unique Fokker streaked green camouflage hand painted with three-inch brushes. The undersurfaces were uniform sky blue. It is believed this plane was assigned to Jasta 6. Compare the horizontal tail shape with that of V.4 and V.5 Coen Smit Collection

A lineup of Dr.Is in early April of 1918, when the German cross marking was being changed from the curved-arm type to the straight arm. Both types of crosses can be seen here, as well as a mix of backgrounds. These Dr.Is are believed to be Jasta 1. Alex Imrie Collection

One of the unarmed Fokker Dr.Is with the Goebel engines assigned to the fighter schools. This is Dr.I 471/17. The training school number is 74. Heinz J. Nowarra Collection

Delivery of the Dr.Is were seriously hampered by a shortage of the 110hp Oberursel Ur.II rotary engine. This was a copy of the 110hp French LeRhone and was actually an improvement because it functioned better on the German substitute motor oil, which the captured French engines could not handle. Eventually it delivered 125hp.

As a result of the oil shortage, some Dr.Is were fitted with such low-powered engines as the 100hp Goebel Goe.II. Such Dr.Is were sent to fighter schools rather than to the front. Approximately fifteen combat Dr.I planes were equipped with captured LeRhone engines at the factory. Others were used as testbeds to evaluate new German engines or captured Allied engines.

Dr.Is began to reach the front lines in the middle of October, but trouble soon appeared. Lt. Heinrich Gontermann, an ace with thirty-nine victories, was stunting serial number 115/17 over his own field when the upper wing broke up and he crashed. Shortly after that, on October 31, Lt. Gunter Pastor suffered a similar fatal accident. These brought officialdom running, along with an order grounding all Fokker triplanes. Inspection of the wings revealed some shoddy work and structural shortcomings that had not been detected in the static test of F.I 101/17. Also, there was poor drainage and inadequate waterproofing of the structure by varnishing. Accumulated moisture quickly caused structural deterioration. Wings were removed from the triplanes and shipped to Fokker for correction. A detailed directive was issued to Fokker outlining the work to be done at his expense. Repaired Dr.Is were back in action after the restriction was lifted, but by then the little triplane had lost its initial appeal as well as its earlier combat advantage. Still, production continued, with the last Dr.I being delivered in May of 1918.

The Dr.Is were replaced at the front with another Fokker, the D.VII biplane, starting in April of 1918. This proved to be, in all probability, the greatest fighter of World War I. The maximum number of Dr.Is at the front was 171 in May 1918, but some sixty-nine were still in service with home-defense and training squadrons at the end of the war.

Manfred von Richthofen returned to action on March 12, 1918. Even though the new Fokker D.VII was available to him, he preferred the Dr.I and used a series of three: serial numbers 114/17, 152/17, and 425/17. One was supposedly fitted for him especially as a gift from Fokker. He used the three to achieve his final seventeen victories (of the eighty total), but was killed in Dr.I 425/17 on April 21, 1918. Controversy still rages as to whether he was shot down by a pursuing Sopwith Camel as he closed in on another Camel ahead of him, or by Australian ground machine guns as he flew low behind the British lines.

The Fokker Dr.Is were mostly gone from the front by June of 1918, but a few were diverted to Germany to test-work with new engines. Some had no change of designation, but at least one was renamed Fokker V. These engine tests were not an attempt to improve the Dr.I as a combat aircraft. Primarily they were to improve the engines themselves, to aid in the development of a supercharger for rotary engines, or to evaluate captured Allied rotary engines, notably the 130hp British Clerget, in a suitable airplane. Three Dr.Is, serial numbers 485/17, 527/17, and 562/17, were used to test the Clergets.

Specifications for the Dr.I included a wingspan of 23ft 7in (7.2m) for the top wing, 20ft 5in (6.2m) for the middle wing, and 18ft 9.5in (5.7m) for the bottom wing. The plane was 18ft 11 in (5.8m) long, and stood 98in (2.5m) high. Powered mainly by the 110hp Oberursel Ur.II nine-cylinder air-cooled rotary engine, it had a top speed of 115mph (185.2km/h), a range of 185mi (297.9km), and a 23,000ft (7012.2m) service ceiling. Twin 7.92mm air-cooled LGM 08/15 machine guns provided adequate armament. The Dr.I weighed 894lb (404.5kg) empty, and grossed out at 1,290lb (583.7kg). Broken down, the gross weight included the 894lb (404.5kg) empty weight, a military load of 130lb (58.8kg), a pilot of 176lb (79.6kg), and fuel and oil at 90lb (40.7kg). The weights for the 110hp LeRhone engine, with the 145hp Oberursel Ur.III, totaled 948lb (429.0kg) empty, and 1,378lb (623.5kg) gross. With the 160hp Goe.III, empty weight was 970lb (438.9kg), gross 1,400lb (633.5kg). And with the 160hp Sh.III empty weight was 1,082lb (489.6kg), while it grossed out at 1,512lb (684.2kg). The Sh.III was a Siemens-Halske engine.

V.6

The V.6 was a parallel development to the V.5, F.I, and Dr.I and reflected Fokker's interest in developing a triplane with a 160hp water-cooled Mercedes engine, which by then was the standard engine for German fighter planes. Because of the heavier engine, the V.6 had slightly larger wings than the V.4, with a span of 26.5ft (8.1m). Since these were a direct scale-up of the V.4, they had correspondingly larger gap and chord.

With the center wing still mounted directly on the top longerons, the lower wing was almost entirely below the fuselage, thus offering a poor wing-fuselage intersection from an aerodynamic standpoint. An attempt was made to correct this by adding fuselage superstructure aft of the lower wing to make a more streamlined installation. Because of the length of the heavier engine, the pilot sat farther behind the center wing than in the Dr.I, and the fuselage was longer.

The V.6 was so poorly designed that the project was dropped, but it made one significant contribution to subsequent Fokker designs that used water-cooled engines: a nose radiator, as used on the French Spads, was positioned immediately behind the propeller but mounted entirely above it. The face of the radiator was angled somewhat as on the German Mercedes automobile instead of being flat, a detail that was to become a trademark of the famed Fokker D.VII.

V.7

Fokker next built four separate near-duplicates of the Dr.I under the V.7 designation. These were attempts to improve the Dr.I through the use of higher-powered rotary engines. Because of the greater weights of these engines, the rear of the fuselage was lengthened some 21.5in (54.6cm) to maintain balance. The test engines had a slightly larger diameter than the standard Oberursel. In order to use the engines without having to build new jigs for a wider fuselage, Fokker simply bulged the engine cowling ahead of the standard-size firewall enough to enclose the larger engine.

No distinction was made between the variously engined V.7s, either by Fokker or the German Air Force. For convenience, they are identified here the way Fokker identified later V-models, in consecutive order by serial number with Roman numeral subscripts: V.7/I, V.7/II, and so on. The first V.7 (constructor number 1788) was powered with the still experimental 160hp Siemens-Halske Sh.III double-acting rotary engine. On this mechanical oddity, the crankshaft rotated at 900rpm in one direction while the cylinders and crankcase rotated at 900rpm in the opposite direction. This gave an engine speed of 1800rpm, quite high by rotary engine standards (the 110hp Oberursel turned at 1200rpm). As a result of this effective 2:1 gearing down, a large area propeller was required, either larger diameter, or four blades instead of two, or both. The V.7/I had a larger-diameter four-bladed propeller and had to have a longer landing gear to accommodate it. This new gear did not use the standard Fokker axle wing.

The V.7/I was entered in the German fighter fly-off competition of January 1918, and turned in outstanding climb and altitude performances during preliminary flights. However, the engine was a long way from being

The Fokker V.6 with the 160hp Mercedes engine, in its original configuration with the lower wing entirely below the fuselage. The cockpit is farther behind the wings than that of previous Fokker triplanes. Heinz J. Nowarra Collection

Modified form of the V.6, with lower superstructure added to fair the lower wing into the fuselage to reduce aerodynamic drag and turbulence. An auxiliary radiator was added to the side of the fuselage, above the landing gear. Alex Imrie Collection

The first of four Fokker V.7s, identified for this book as V.7/I. Note the bulged cowling for the larger Siemens-Halske double-acting rotary engine, the lengthened rear fuselage, and the larger-diameter four-bladed propeller that required a longer landing gear without the trademark Fokker axle wing. Willi Stiasni Collection

ready for service and the V.7/I was eliminated. Had the engine been ready for combat, the career of the fighting Fokker triplane might have been extended. Re-engined with an Oberursel, the V.7/I was redesignated Dr.I and given serial number 120/17.

The final Fokker V.7, the V.7/IV that was sent to Austria-Hungary for a 1918 fighter plane competition. Obvious is the bulged cowling for the Steyr engine, and the lengthened rear fuselage characteristic of the high-powered V.7s. Courtesy Franz Selinger

The second V.7, V.7/II (constructor number 1830), was used to test a 160hp Gnome engine. Whether this was a captured example of the new single-row French 160hp Gnome as used in the Nieuport 28 or the twin-row fourteen-cylinder Oberursel Ur.III rotary engine, or even the twin-row Gnome copy previously used on the Fokker E.IV or D.III, is not known. The German Oberursel copy of the Gnome was sometimes referred to as Gnome in official German documents.

V.7/III, the third V.7 (constructor number 1919), was a testbed for the new 170hp Goebel Goe.III engine. It demonstrated superior climb and altitude performances at the January fighter competition. As with the Siemens in the V.7/I, the Goebel was far from being perfected and the V.7/III was withdrawn. Later when mated with a standard Oberursel, it was designated as a Dr.I and given serial number 599/17.

The last V.7, V.7/IV (constructor number 1981), was shipped without an engine to the Ungarische Allgemeine Maschinenfabrik AG (MAG), an Austro-Hungarian aircraft manufacturer in which Fokker had acquired an interest. Here it was fitted with a 145hp Steyr rotary engine, an improved Austro-Hungarian copy of the equivalent French LeRhone. The V.7/IV given the Austro-Hungarian serial number 90.03, proved to be superior to the standard 110hp Dr.I in early test flights. Unfortunately for Fokker, a factory

The Hansa-Brandenburg CC flying boat, known as the Kampf Dreidecker Wasser, was a single adaptation of the biplane designed by Ernest Heinkel in late 1916. The wing radiator indicates it was a late-model CC built during 1917.

The bottom wing was shortened and a third wing was added at the intersection of the star struts. It was unsuccessful and ended up as another wasted effort. Bowers Collection

test pilot damaged it in a landing accident and it was not repaired in time for the Austro-Hungarian fighter competition held in July of 1918.

Hansa-Brandenburg Triplanes

CC

This design was developed for the Hansa und Brandenburgische Flugzeugwerke by Ernst Heinkel in 1918, from a 1916 CC flying boat fighter. The CC flying boat was called that in honor of Camillo Castiglione, who owned the firm. The Austro-Hungarian Navy designated it the KDW (Kampf Doppeldecker Wasser (fighter water biplane), so the triplane would naturally have been the Kampf Dreidecker Wasser had it been adopted by the Navy. It was at least given the Navy serial number A.45.

The triplane incorporated the star strut, the unique crossed-strut interplane bracing system of the CC. It was essentially the standard CC biplane design, with a slightly shortened bottom wing and a small center wing inserted at the junction point of the star struts. The hull was lengthened and the radiator was mounted on the top wing. The wooden hull was well streamlined and had a step underneath. The wing-tip floats were also streamlined and attached to the lower wing by a single strut in front and two struts at the rear.

Specifications:

Powerplant, 185hp Austro-Daimler engine; span 30.5ft (9.3m); length 25ft (7.6m).

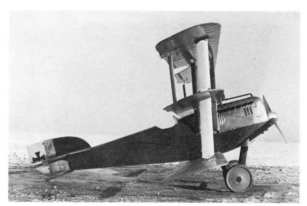

A perfect profile photo of the Hansa-Brandenburg L.16 single-seat fighter plane developed from scratch for the Austro-Hungarian K.u.K Luftstreikrafte late in the war. Even a number of modifications could not save the design, so it was dropped. Note the huge airfoil section, I-type interplane bracing struts, and the solid appearance they gave to the plane. Bowers Collection

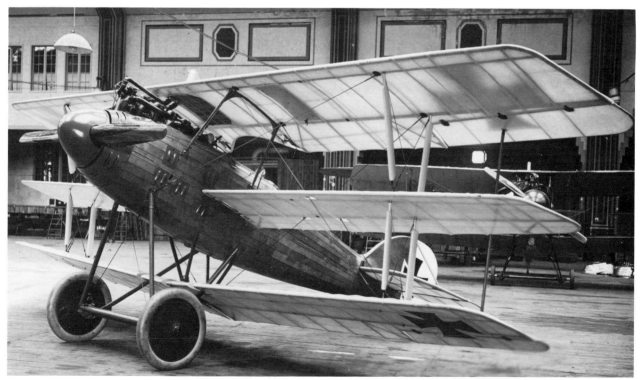

The LFG Roland Dr.I or D.IV was developed by the Luftfahrzeug Gesellschaft mbH by converting the D.IV biplane to a triplane. The fuselage used the "clinker-built" ship-lap construction found only on Roland designs. Other major changes included the rearrangement of the center section struts, and longer landing gear to get the wheels clear of the deeply underslung bottom wing. Bowers Collection

L-16

The L-16 was a relatively conventional triplane fighter designed from scratch by Ernst Heinkel at a fairly late date, because it used a letter-and-number identification instead of the letters-only system followed by Heinkel with his other H-B designs. A number of the German H-B Models were built in Austria by the Phonix firm; the L-16 is listed among others in official records as a Phonix. While it is possible that the L-16 may have gone into production in that country, it is more logical to assume that the single German prototype was sent there for evaluation, and went no further.

Specifications:

Powerplant 185hp Austro-Daimler engine; span 29.5ft (9.0m); top speed 117.8mph (189.7km/h).

LFG Roland Dr.I Triplane

The Luftfahrzeug Gesellschaft mbH, called Roland, produced an experimental triplane in 1917, the D.IV, which was the first airplane to use a new construction method on its fuselage. The *Klinkerrumpf* system consisted of long, tapered lengths of wood, fixed longitudinally to the framework of formers and longerons. This actually was a true "clinker" in the shipbuilding sense, since the strips did overlap as they did in boat building. Some called this method *Lap-Strake*; take your choice.

Apparently this single model, after a crash, was rebuilt since two different types have been identified in photographs. The prototype crashed in September of 1917. It appears that the fuselage of an experimental biplane was used because some photos of the prototype show the fillet for the bottom wing—ours do not. Since the bottom wing of the triplane was mounted on a pylon there was no reason for the fillet, other than a quick conversion to test the design.

The Lohner Dr.I, an Austrian design developed from a biplane by Jakob Lohner AG in Vienna. The Dr.I was powered by an Austro-Daimler 185hp engine. The fuselage was of plywood, with an unusually long dorsal fin that combined with the pilot's headrest. The elevator was patterned after the German Albatros type. Notice how clean the engine cowling is. Bowers Collection

Rear view of the Dr.I shows the one-piece elevator, the variance in length and wing tips, and the unusual strut arrangement: The upper struts slope inward at a forty-five-degree angle to the center wing, and outward from the center wing to the lower. Bowers Collection

The Roland Dr.I was powered by a Daimler-Mercedes 160hp engine. Except for the fuselage, it was a conventional design. The horizontal stabilizer could be adjusted on the ground.

Lohner Triplane

The Lohner Dr.I was an Austrian experimental triplane developed from the existing Lohner D-type biplane by the Jakob Lohner AG in 1917. The fuselage was a slab-sided plywood type. A large and long dorsal fin ran from the rear of the plane to terminate at the pilot's headrest. A straight-across elevator, similar to that used on the Albatros, and a small rudder comprised the tail section. The arrangement of the wing struts was a departure from most practices in that the upper struts sloped inward nearly forty-five degrees to the center wing, while the lower struts sloped outward from the center wing at the same angle. The design was unsuccessful, and was abandoned like so many others.

Specifications:

Powerplant, 185hp Austro-Daimler; span 28.5ft (8.7m); length 21ft 9.5in (6.6m); wing area 226sq-ft (21.0sq-m); gross weight 2,037lb (921.7kg); top speed 110mph (177.1km/h).

Nieuport Triplanes

The Nieuport Company was founded in 1909 by Edouard de Nieport as the Societe Anonyme des Establissment Nieuport at Issy-les-Moulineaux, Paris. Just why the company was named Nieuport when the founder's name was de Nieport is not known, but together with his brother Charles they designed a number of monoplanes prior to World War I. Edouard died in a crash in 1911, and Charles was killed in 1913 in another flying accident. The company continued building airplanes and in 1914 hired a young naval designer named Gustave Delage, who was responsible for the wartime designs.

Nieuport produced a number of prototype triplanes early in the war, but none were successful. Delage favored small, highly maneuverable airplanes so he liked the triplane idea. It offered the possibility of shortening the wingspan and length. However, others had learned that there was an inherent hazard in triplane designs: The air flowing over the lower wings would be forced against the upper wing, thus placing a dangerous stress on it. Delage decided to stagger the wings to eliminate this stress. The rigging of the triplane's three wings was extremely difficult and the lateral stability was marginal. It was difficult to land and was sluggish in turns. Two versions were tried, one with the top wing staggered forward, and the other with the top wing staggered to the rear. The latter had a spinner attached to the propeller shaft to decrease drag. Both were powered by a 110hp LeRhone and had a speed range of 120–125mph (193.2–201.3km/h). Neither version ever went into production, however.

One of three different types of Nieuport triplanes. This is the only one with the wings staggered to the rear, and the only one to have a spinner on the propeller hub. Frank A. Thorell Collection of the National Air Museum

The British received two of the three triplanes that had been produced in January of 1917. One was sent to Aircraft Depot No. 2 at Candas as N1388 for evaluation by the Royal Flying Corps (RFC) which assigned serial number A6686. After testing at Candas it was sent to Martlesham Heath in England for further evaluation, but proved to be unacceptable and was dropped by the RFC.

The other triplane was given to the Royal Naval Air Service (RNAS) in March of 1917. It had wings similar to those on A6686. The RNAS applied serial number N521 to replace the Nieuport number N1946.

The Nieuport two-seat observation version had the wings staggered to the front. The engine was an 80hp LeRhone. Nieuport serial number N1118 was applied to the rudder. The

Eiffel Tower in the background indicates that this field was close to Paris. Frank A. Thorell Collection of the National Air Museum

This Nieuport was the one sent to the RFC in January of 1917 and assigned serial number A6686. It was tested at Martlesham Heath, England, and found to be very unstable.

Pictured here in RFC markings at Orfordness. Bowers Collection

The Oesterrische Flugzeugfabrik AG of Austria, known as Oeffag, designed and built this Dr.I which was powered by a 200hp Austro-Daimler engine. It was a typical Austrian wooden aircraft with a plywood-covered fuselage. The empennage resembled that of the German Albatros D.II and D.III which Oeffag built under license. Bowers Collection

It, too, had first been sent to Candas Aircraft Depot No. 2. It was flown to Hounslow on February 9, 1917, and then was sent to RNAS Depot Dunkerque on March 29, 1917. The second plane differed from the first in having ailerons with regular taper, not the usual inverse taper. It also had a different engine, a 130hp Clerget. This model was also deemed unsuitable and was abandoned by the RNAS.

Oeffag Triplane

The Oesterrische Flugzeugfabrik AG, otherwise known as Oeffag, originally manufactured the C-I two-seat models, and the German Albatros under license undertook to build the Austrian government's official design, a new triplane designated as the Oeffag Dr.I.

It was a typical Austrian wooden construction, featuring plywood covering for the fuselage. One of the unconventional features was the difference in gap between the wings: There was a greater difference between the top wing and center wing than between the center and lower wing. The horizontal tail bore a strong resemblance to that of the Albatros. The top wing was continuous, while the center and bottom wings were halved. The center wing halves were attached to the fuselage and the bottom wing was attached to the undercarriage struts and held together by rods. A single interplane strut on each side held all three wings together. Four cabane struts held the top wing to the fuselage.

Despite the added wire rigging, the entire wing structure seemed questionable. The Dr.I was not pursued by the Austrian government and did not go into production.

Pfalz Triplanes

The Pfalz Flugzeug Werke built Roland fighters under license before taking the plunge and producing designs and aircraft of their own. Their designer Rudolf Gehringer produced the Pfalz D.III, a strong, streamlined, and better-built plane. At the time of the triplane craze, they got into the act by converting their biplane into a three-winger. Everything but the wings were the standard Pfalz D.III, and even the wing struts followed the one-piece laminated wood construction of the D.III. No factory designation was ever assigned to this experimental triplane.

Pfalz followed up with a radically new design, and designated it the Dr.I since it had been designed as a triplane from the beginning. The clean, compact

In this profile view, the difference is obvious in the gap between the top and middle wing. Notice how much closer the gap between the center and bottom wing is. Since most triplanes used equal-size gaps between all three wings, this Oeffag design is unconventional. Peter M. Grosz Collection

airplane was designed by Ernst Eversbusch. The powerplant was an eleven-cylinder 160hp Siemens-Halske Sh.III geared rotary engine enclosed in a circular aluminum cowl in which twelve holes had been cut to provide cooling. The upper portion was removable to provide access without having to remove the propeller. The propeller was large and coarse pitched to make the best use of the slow rpm of the Sh.III engine. The wings were hollow box spars, with three-ply ribs attached and covered with fabric. The wings varied in span and chord; the top wing was largest and carried the equal-chord ailerons. The center wing was smallest. The fuselage was a plywood monocoque built up of wooden frames reinforced by ply gussets, giving the whole piece a thick cross section. The fin was built into the fuselage's rear. Rudder and elevator were fabric covered. Twin un-synchronized Spandau machine guns were mounted in front of the cockpit.

Baron Manfred von Richthofen was asked to flight test the Pfalz Dr.I and went to Speyer-am-Rhein in Bavaria to do so, but was disappointed to find it was inferior to the Fokker Dr.I and therefore did not recommend it for mass production. A total of ten Pfalz Dr.Is were built and a few may have actually been flown in combat, making it the third triplane to be manufactured during the war. Two other projected Pfalz Dr-models, the Dr.II to have been powered by a 100hp Oberursel and the Dr.IIa using a 110hp Siemens-Halske Sh.I, were deemed unsatisfactory and were dropped.

Sablatnig Triplane

Dr. Joseph Sablatnig formed the Sablatnig Flugzeugbau GmbH in October of 1915. After winning a competition to build a floatplane fighter, the company received an order to manufacture two, thus assuring him of a chance to build his business.

The first Pfalz triplane was simply an attempt to modify the standard D.III biplane by adding a third wing between the biplane wings. The D.III-type struts were retained. This prototype is reported never to have been flown. Peter M. Grosz Collection

The Pfalz Dr.I (serial 3050/17), designed by Ernst Eversbusch, was the only other German triplane to be put into production—despite the fact that Baron von Richthofen tested it and rejected it in December 1917. It was perhaps the cleanest of all German triplane designs. Observe the unique cowling around the eleven-cylinder Siemens-Halske double-acting rotary engine. Alex Imrie Collection

The Pfalz Dr.II was a Dr.I airframe mated to the 140hp eleven-cylinder Oberursel engine as an alternate to the Siemens. The Dr.I in the background has redesigned cowling louvers and the bottom segment removed. Alex Imrie Collection

Early Pfalz Dr.I, with the larger cowling apertures. Later Dr.Is had the bottom quarter of the cowl removed. The outer struts resemble a Y. Bowers Collection

Sablatnig's first effort was the SF2, which did not live up to his expectations. His next design, the SF4 in the biplane stage, was completed and sent to the SVK for testing and approval, but again was found wanting in rate of climb and maneuverability. He then decided to turn the second SF4, which was then under construction, into the triplane format to improve the rate of climb and increase maneuverability.

This version had I-form interplane struts like the Fokker, and ailerons on all three wings interconnected by a single strut on each set of wings. The center wing was divided in the middle and attached to the fuselage and upper wing by I-struts. Armament consisted of a single synchronized machine gun firing forward through the propeller arc. Twin floats were fitted, making the SF4 the only seaplane of World War I designed as a triplane fighter. The SF4 was powered by a Benz 150hp engine. The span was 30ft 1.5in (9.2m), and length totaled 27ft 2.5in (8.3m). Wing area was 306sq-ft (28.4sq-m). The wings had a slight forward stagger, but were all of equal span.

These planes were assembled in the works courtyard on the Koepenckerstrasse in Berlin. Since the plant was almost in the center of the city, it made any flight testing impossible. Sablatnig had tested them on a small dockyard at Muggelsee for waterworthiness, so it is no surprise that their designs failed to meet the requirements and were rejected.

V. Saveliev Triplane

This was a Russian triplane of World War I vintage that was used at the Moscow Military Aerodrome for training. It was a slab-sided triplane which in profile looked like a quadruplane because of the floating aileron that extended beneath the lower wing and covered the same span as the wing. The triplane wings were staggered forward. The gear and tail skid were extra long to keep the aileron from dragging on the ground. It had a rotary engine and comma-type vertical tail.

Schutte-Lanz Triplane

The Schutte-Lanz Dr.I triplane prototype of 1917 was a product of the firm of the same name. They were more noted for building wood-frame airships and other

The Sablatnig SF4 was one of a kind. Two aircraft were built: one was a biplane, the other was a triplane. The triplane had twin floats. Due to the added wing area, the triplane's wings were 9ft 2in shorter than the biplane's. Wingspan was 30ft 1¹/₂in (9.2m), length was 27ft 2¹/₂in (8.3m), and wing area was 306sq-ft. (28.4sq-m). Power was supplied by a 150hp Benz engine. Joseph Nieto Collection

German aircraft under license. In the early days, sooner or later every company involved in aviation tried their hand at designing a triplane, and Schutte-Lanz was no exception.

The Schutte-Lanz Dr.I prototype of 1917, even though not adopted by the German Air Force, still received the official Dr.I designation. It was simply another adaptation of an existing biplane and was almost identical to the D.I biplane. Schutte-Lanz was more well known for its zeppelin-like wooden-frame airships. There appears to be a Gotha bomber in the background. Coen Smit Collection

Their first attempt was the experimental D.I biplane. Naturally, like most others, they converted it into a triplane. All components except the wings were almost identical to the D.I. The main differences were the N-struts and the heavy stagger between the center wing and the bottom wing; there was no stagger between the center and top wing. Although given an official Dr.I designation, the plane did not bring in a production contract and went the way of so many others.

Siemens-Schuckert Triplane

Siemens-Schuckert was a large German electrical firm that was world famous back in the 1900s and still is today. In 1907 they became involved in the aeronautical field as a manufacturer of nonrigid airships. Two years later they tried building airplanes, but this attempt did not produce any significant results so the branch was closed in 1911, only to be reopened at the outbreak of war. Designers Franz and Bruno Steffen, and Forssman turned out a series of large bombers, called the Riesenflugzeug, or "giant aircraft." This R-series was successful. Eventually they turned to fighters and designed several successful planes. Finally, as had many other companies, they tried their design skills on a triplane in 1917. The Dr.I was completed in July of 1917 and underwent a long series of tests over an extended period of time.

The Dr.I utilized a D.I fuselage and a Siemens-Halske Sh.I engine and was rebuilt with an increased

The Schutte-Lanz Dr.I was powered by the 160hp Mercedes. Note the use of N-type struts, and the heavy stagger between the center and bottom wing. There is no stagger between the center and top wing. Alex Imrie Collection

60

wing area after a crash. Another Dr.II with an Sh.III engine and a D.IIB fuselage was scrapped during construction. The DDr.I was called the "Flying Egg" because of its fuselage nacelle. The design had been submitted to the Idflieg (the inspector of flying troops) in June of 1917 and accepted. The twin tractor-pusher

Called the "Flying Egg," the Siemens-Schuckert DDr.I was the first twin-engine fighter airplane, but crashed on its first test flight. It also was the first push-pull type engine. The rear engine had a four-bladed propeller while the nose engine had a standard two-bladed one. Technically, this could not be called a twin-engine plane because the engine installations did not match. Powered by Siemens-Halske engines of 130hp each, the triplane had a wing area of 323sq-ft (30.0 sq-m) and a gross weight of 2,000lb (905.0kg). Heinz J. Nowarra Collection

The DDr.I's twin tail booms, elevator and rudders, strut, and rear engine mounting. Heinz J. Nowarra Collection

The prototype British Sopwith Tripehound was essentially the famous 80hp Sopwith Pup fitted with three wings and a

130hp Clerget engine. It had a single Vickers gun for armament. Bowers Collection engines were Sh. Ia types. The rear engine had a four-bladed propeller while the forward one carried a two-bladed type. Technically this engine arrangement cannot be called a twin-engine mount since the installations did not match. The twin-boom tail unit was a throwback to the pusher scouts of 1915. Unfortunately, it was destroyed on its first flight in a crash in November 1917. An intended follow-on model to have been powered by two Sh. II engines, the DDr. II, was canceled. The extra D in the Dr designation probably was used to indicate the model had two engines.

Specifications:

Powerplants, two Sh. Ia 130hp engines; wing area 323sq-ft (30.0sq-m); gross weight 2,000lb (905.0kg).

Sopwith Triplanes

The Sopwith Aviation Company of Kingston-on-Thames, England, was the world's second most prolific developer of triplane designs after Curtiss, but it built only one significant production model. That was the 130hp unnumbered triplane fighter nicknamed Tripehound, or simply Tripe. It was a very good fighter for the time, and served as an inspiration for the flock of German and Allied triplane fighter prototypes that appeared in late 1917 and early 1918.

The Tripehound was not Sopwith's first triplane, however; six different Sopwith three-wingers were built during the war. The three larger models are described in chapter 4.

Clerget Triplane

The Tripehound, the only production Allied triplane fighter and the most famous, was a three-wing adaptation of the famous Pup. The Pup was an 80hp single-seater that was basically a scaled-down Sopwith 1½-strutter two-seater. The single-seat fighter was so similar that it was initially referred to as the Strutter's Pup. The nickname stuck, became official, and started the Sopwith tradition of giving its planes animal names.

Introduced in the spring of 1916, the triplane was in effect a Pup beefed up to take a 130hp Clerget engine and three wings that had the same 26ft (7.9m) span as the Pup. The purpose of three wings was not so much to make a more maneuverable airplane, but to improve the pilot's visibility by decreasing the chord of the wings. The narrow wing used single struts. Flying loads were taken by only two wires on each side from the bottom longeron to the upper wing; the single landing wire on each side passed through the center wing.

Some aerodynamic inefficiency, not fully appreciated at the time, involved the center wing. It was located nearly 1ft (30.5cm) above the upper longerons and even above the forward superstructure, and ended at the center section struts. This left a gap across the fuselage and in effect two more wingtips, with subsequent disruption of lift and generation of turbulent airflow. These problems were of little consequence on the Tripe; however, they caused serious trouble on the next Sopwith triplane.

With the added power, the Clerget triplane proved to be a more than satisfactory fighter. It was

One of the Sopwith Tripehounds that was captured intact by the Germans at Adlershof in July 1917. It was one of the earlier planes, and had the original large tail planes. The

Tripehound helped inspire the boom in German triplane fighter development. Bowers Collection

ordered into production for both the RNAS and the RFC. The RFC, however, never received its triplanes; for some reason they were exchanged for British-built French Spad VIIs. In an unusual move, the first RNAS example was sent to the front in June of 1916 for combat evaluation, and was sent off on a mission within fifteen minutes of its arrival.

The Sopwiths reached the front in squadron strength by February 1917. They served effectively with four RNAS squadrons, No. 1, No. 8, No. 9, and No. 10. In the absence of an official name or model designation, the triplane was referred to by the diminutive term Tripe, or the more formal Tripehound. Fast and maneuverable, the new Sopwith had one notable shortcoming—a single .303cal machine gun for armament at a time when the new German models were carrying two guns. In the interest of increased maneuverability, the area of the horizontal tail was reduced. The Pup configuration, in which the leading edge was longer than the trailing edge, was shortened for a reduction of 10sq-ft (0.93sq-m).

The combat career of the Tripe was short, barely seven months. By the time it was replaced by the two-gun Sopwith Camel, however, it had made its mark.

Flt. Sub.-Lt. Raymond Collishaw of Naval No. 10, one of Canada's leading aces, scored sixteen victories in twenty-seven days and his "Black Flight" racked up eighty-seven victories in less than three months. They had named their planes *Black Maria, Black Prince, Black Roger, Black Sheep,* and *Black Death.* On the negative side, at least two Tripehounds were forced down intact behind enemy lines, to initiate the officially sponsored boom in German triplane fighter prototypes.

There were 145 Tripehounds built by Sopwith, Clayton and Shuttleworth, Limited, and Oakley and Company, Limited. These planes were assigned Sopwith serials: N500, N504, N524, N5420–5494 (75), N6290–6309 (20). Clayton and Shuttleworth serials included: N533–538 (6), and N5350–5389 (40). Oakley

numbers were N5910–5912 (3) and N5913–5934 (22). These add up to 169, but 24 were eventually canceled.

Two original Tripehounds still survive today, one at the Royal Air Force (RAF) Museum in England, and one in Russia. Several fully flyable replicas have been built in the current replica movement. (See chapter 8.)

Specifications:

Span 26.5ft (8.1m); length 19ft 10in (6.0m); wing area 231sq-ft (21.4sq-m); gross weight 1,415lb (1640.3kg); top speed 119mph (191.6km/h) (N504) at 10,000ft (3,048.8m); rate of climb to 10,000ft 10 minutes 36 seconds.

Hispano Triplane

Testing of the Clerget-engine Tripehound was followed by the building of two slightly larger single-seat triplanes powered by French Hispano-Suiza water-cooled V-8 engines. One had a 200hp geared engine (N510) and the other a 150hp direct-drive (N509). Where the Tripehound owed much of its detail to the 1½-Strutter, particularly in the size of such components as the tail and landing gear, the Hispano-Suiza was larger and differed slightly, but was actually a whole new design. Apparently, the two planes were tested without ever carrying armament. Climb performance was excellent, but there were problems. Turbulence, possibly resulting from the inner open ends of the center wing, caused the tail of the 200hp model to break off in flight in December of 1916 at Eastchurch. The 150hp model also had tail flutter due to the turbulence problem and was withdrawn from service in October of 1917.

Perhaps the one significant contribution of the Hispano triplane to subsequent British design was its use of a flat-nose radiator behind the propeller, with an opening for the shaft.

Two prototypes of slightly larger Sopwith single-seat triplanes—powered with 150hp and 200hp French Hispano-Suiza engines—were built and tested but never put into production. Bowers Collection

The third of three Sopwith Snark fighters during tests in 1919. The large propeller spinner formed a smooth nose for the new ABC radial engine. Note the continuity of the center wing across the fuselage. Imperial War Museum, London

Specifications:

Span 26.5ft (8.1m); length 23ft 2in (7.1m); top speed 120mph (193.2km/h); rate of climb to 10,000ft (3,048.8m) at 9 minutes.

Snark Triplane

The single-seat Snark fighter, ordered in early 1918, was not a new design but essentially a three-wing adaptation of the second Sopwith Snail prototype of late 1917. The notable new feature of both Snail models was the use of the 170hp All British Motors Company Wasp, a seven-cylinder air-cooled radial engine. The first Snail had a conventional four-longeron fuselage, but the second had a plywood-covered semimonocoque fuselage. The Snark used this feature, plus the Snail's landing gear and tail surface, but a 360hp ABC Dragonfly nine-cylinder radial engine powered the plane.

The triplane wings were conventional two-spar types with parallel interplane struts. An oddity here was that the struts between the upper and lower wing did not form a straight line with the lower struts, the stagger of the struts of the upper wing relative to the center wing was less than that of the center wing-lower wing combination. Ailerons were fitted to all three wings. The lesson of the Hispano triplane seemed to have been learned. The center wing was now continuous above the top of the fuselage and at the pilot's eye level.

Armament was unusual for the time in that two synchronized .303cal Vickers machine guns were mounted on the fuselage, along with four unsynchronized Lewis guns which were mounted in pairs and placed below the lower wing. In view of the need to replace the drums of the Lewis guns in flight, this would seem to have been a poor arrangement but may have only been meant to provide a more lethal burst of fire in the right situation.

Three Snark prototypes were ordered, with RAF serials F4068–4070. The first airframe was not available until December. Chronic engine problems de-

layed installation until the spring of 1918 and official testing did not begin until September. The other two Snarks were completed by the end of 1919. Serial F4068 was returned to Sopwith for engine work, and was not returned to the RAF until April of 1920.

Whether or not the Snark would have been a good fighter was a moot point since the war was over, and the Sopwith Snipe remained the principal RAF fighter for several more years. The main thing that the Snark and its contemporaries with the ABC engines accomplished was to prove that the high-powered static radial engine was not yet a serviceable powerplant.

Specifications:

Span 26.5ft (8.1m); length 20.5ft (6.3m); wing area 322sq-ft (29.9sq-m); top speed 130mph (209.3km/h).
Note: On April 1, 1918, the RNAS and RFC merged to form the new RAF. Serial numbers for the two original services assigned by the Ministry of Munitions had by that time reached E1600. All subsequent serial numbers are RAF assignments.

Swedish Triplanet

The Triplanet was never given an official name by the Swedish Army, but has been called the Thulin triplane, the Kjellson, or the Kjellson-von Parat triplane in the literature. It was an original Swedish design assembled from spare parts and the fuselage of a salvaged Thulin I. The plane was powered by a Swedish version of the LeRhone engine built under license as the Thulin Model A. Henry Kjellson was an engineer, while C. G. von Parat was a pilot. Both of these pioneers were quite well known in Swedish aviation circles at that time.

The fuselage of the Thulin I was covered by clear-varnished birch plywood and was left in that state when used in building the triplane. However, the turtle deck was covered by clear-doped fabric. The engine cowling and fuel tank were aluminum. The wheel spreader bar was also clear-varnished birch plywood. Wings, tail planes, and wheel covers were covered by clear-doped linen. Power was supplied by the 90hp Thulin Model A nine-cylinder air-cooled rotary engine fitted with a mahogany propeller. The plane was called the "Galosh Rack" by some of the mechanics and pilots.

The three-crown Swedish national insignia was applied in black to both the top and bottom wings as well as to both sides of the fuselage. The Swedish man-of-war flag was applied to both sides of the rudder. Originally, it was blue with a yellow cross, though it doesn't show in any of the photos. The fuselage markings were on a white field.

The Triplanet's first test flight took place at Malmstatt (Malmen) on September 18, 1918, with Lt. Nils Rodehn, an experienced pilot, at the controls. The test of approximately fifteen minutes was enough to prove the soundness of the design. The plane, which had been built at Malmstatt, remained there while a number of test flights were conducted, all of which were successful.

The Sopwith Hispano was another undesignated Sopwith fighter, similar to the Tripehound but actually a new design built around the 150hp Hispano-Suiza V-8 engine. Only two prototypes were built. Bowers Collection

Swedish Triplanet, in a perfect profile position (almost). This photo shows the sturdiness of the design and the width of the interplane struts. Nils-Arne Nilsson Collection

The plane's serial number 831 applied to the fuselage had a special significance: the 8 stood for the year it was built, and the 31 indicated it was the thirty-first aircraft built in the Central Workshop in Malmen. Today, the Swedish Air Force Museum is located in Malmstatt.

The career of the Triplanet came to an abrupt end at 8:15am on the morning of April 12, 1919, when two young lieutenants took off on a routine flight. The plane had not been flown for a month; for some unknown reason, the instructor was flying the plane from the front seat, which he had never done before. The takeoff was normal, but the plane quickly turned back toward the field. At the southeastern corner of the field it was only about 656ft (200m) high when suddenly it went into a 90deg left bank, lost speed, and spun into the ground. The plane was a total loss, and Lt. Folke Soderlind was killed instantly. Lt. Gosta Carlsson died a short time later. These men were the nineteenth and twentieth Swedish aviators to lose their lives in aerial accidents. Kjellson and von Parat were quite distraught over the crash; some believed it may have been due to faulty construction.

Specifications:

Span 29.5ft (9m); length 21ft 3.8in (6.5m); wing area 258.6sq-ft (24sq-m); height 9ft 10in (3m); top speed 93mph (149.7km/h) (approximately); gross weight 1,981lb (900kg); service ceiling 12,464ft (3,800m); endurance 2.5 hours; rate of climb to 3,280ft

(1,000m) six minutes; range 155.3mi (250km); and landing speed 43.5mph (70km/h). (The landing gear was placed well forward to prevent ground loops.)

WKF Triplane

The Wiener Karosserie und Flugzeugfabrik (Viennese Car and Airplane Works) developed a new fighter in late 1917. The D.I prototype was a biplane that gave rise to the Dr.I triplane. The triplane fuselage

These men are believed to be Lt. Gosta Carlsson and Lt. Folke Soderlind, who were both killed in aerial accidents. The helmet under the left arm of the pilot seems to be a rigid-type crash helmet rather than just a head covering meant for warmth. Nils-Arne Nilsson Collection

featured nonparallel plywood sides converging down-ward to a V-shaped bottom, but had a rounded top. The instrument panel was placed so far forward that to enable the pilot to read them, a pair of small round windows had to be cut in the coaming to provide enough light for the pilot to read his instruments. The Dr.I underwent a limited test period and was dropped in favor of the biplane.

Specifications:

Powerplant, 200hp Austro-Daimler; span 26ft 2in (8.0m); length 29ft 7in (9.0m); wing area 242sq-ft (22.5sq-m); gross weight 2,060lb (932.1kg).

The end of serial number 831, and the end of Swedish triplanes. The black crowns on the upper wing are national insignias. No attempt was made to salvage the parts, for obvious reasons. Nils-Arne Nilsson Collection

An excellent view of the Triplanet's struts and sturdy landing gear. You can also see the ailerons on the upper and center wing. Nils-Arne Nilsson Collection

The Viennese Car and Airplane Works developed both biplane and triplane fighter versions, as had become a common practice by 1917. The fuselage was unorthodox, having nonparallel sides tapering downward to blend with the V-shaped bottom. The turtle deck was rounded. Small round windows were cut out just ahead of or below the cockpit to provide enough light for the pilot to read the instrument panel, which was placed far forward of the cockpit cutout. Bowers Collection

Front view showing the well-cowled Austro-Daimler 200hp engine, the top-wing-mounted radiator, the four-bladed propeller, and the winglet-type spreader bar. The span was 26ft 2in (8.0m), length was 29ft 7in (9.0m), and wing area totaled 242sq-ft (22.5sq-m). The plane grossed out at 2,060lb (932.1kg). It never went into production. Bowers Collection

Chapter 4

Larger World War I Triplanes

Both sides developed larger triplanes, entirely separate from the single-seaters, ranging from two-seater observation planes to four- and five-engined bombers and flying boats. Development of these types began in mid-1915, and resulted in some designs that at the time were the world's largest airplanes.

The term world's largest airplane requires some clarification. Generally people tend to think of the biggest airplane in terms of its wingspan, but other factors of equal importance are wing area and gross weight. Either can make a plane with slightly less wingspan seem "bigger" than one with a greater span. At times, all three criteria existed in the same aircraft to create the undisputed "largest airplane in the world."

While triplane fighter production was limited to Sopwith Tripehound and Fokker Dr.I, production of large-size triplanes was even more limited as only one of the larger designs—the unique twin-fuselage Italian Caproni Ca.40 series—attained production status.

AEG Triplane

Two experimental observation two-seaters, one a biplane, the other a triplane, were built under the same model number C.VIII, by the Allgemeine Elektrizitats Gesellschaft (AEG). The triplane was basically a biplane with the wings relocated far enough apart to permit a third wing to be fitted between them. An extra strut was installed at the midpoint of each panel for stiffness. It was powered by the 200hp Benz engine.

Armstrong-Whitworth Triplanes

The Armstrong-Whitworth F.K.12 was a three-seat fighter designed by the British firm of Sir W.G. Armstrong-Whitworth Company Limited of Gosforth. It was developed late in 1915, before Allied fighters were equipped with machine-gun synchronizers to meet the Fokker menace.

The armament arrangement of the F.K.12—the letters identified the design as one of Frederick

The AEG C.VIII was a clean design. The two-seater observation plane was pretty standard. A couple of unique features, though, were its exhaust stack, which was moved back under the center wing, and the unusual strut fastening to the lower wing. The outline of the top wing has been enhanced. Heinz J. Nowarra Collection

Koolhoven, the Dutch-born designer—was rather unique. In the initial version, two machine gunners were stationed in the front of the long nacelles which were mounted on the top of the long-span center wing. On the redesigned version, shorter nacelles were located under the center wing. On the original version the main landing gear had a single pair of wheels close together under the centerline of the fuselage, with a small outrigger wheel under the lower wing tips to maintain lateral balance and prevent ground loops. The production version reverted to a more conventional arrangement. The engine for both versions was the Rolls-Royce water-cooled V-12, the forerunner of the Rolls-Royce Eagle.

A production order was placed for three F.K.12s, RFC serial numbers 7838–7841, but only 7838 is known to have been delivered; the development of a suitable Allied gun synchronizer had eliminated the need for this type of fighter.

BFW Triplane

The BFW N-1 triplane was developed by Bayrische Flugzeugwerke AG, the Bavarian branch of the well-known Albatros company. The firm had been building the Hannover CL-V biplane under license, but was sufficiently independent to work on experimental designs of its own. The N-1 was designed as a night bomber, as identified by the prefix N. Only the prototype was built. Several features other than its large size are notable, including the wide biplane tail,

which was reminiscent of the Hannover, two separate dual-wheel landing gear trucks, and a radiator mounted high on the center section struts.

Since this triplane was produced near the end of the war little information is available on it. Possibly it was destroyed at the end of the war to prevent the Allies from making use of it.

Bristol Triplanes

Captain F. S. Barnwell, spurred by public demand for a bomber capable of raiding Berlin in retaliation for

View of the box-like nacelles housing the gunners on the Armstrong-Whitworth F.K.12, four-bladed propeller, wing-tip skids, strut arrangement, and double-wheel trucks. Bowers Collection

The Albatros Bavarian branch had a few experimental designs, including this BFW N-1 night bomber triplane. Features included a biplane horizontal tail, separate dual- wheel trucks, and radiator positioned on the center section struts. Heinz J. Nowarra Collection

German air raids on London, submitted a design for a B.1 four-engine triplane bomber on October 10, 1917. The layout was passed on to W. T. Reid for detailing. Reid used a flat-sided fuselage that was reinforced by spruce compression members and braced by swaged tie rods for ease in construction. Four engines were mounted in tandem pairs on the center wing. The prototype was completed in August 1918 with four 230hp Siddeley Puma engines in lieu of the proposed Rolls-Royce 360hp Eagles, which were not available in time.

The first prototype British Bristol Braemar Mk.I was complete in August of 1918 with four 230hp Siddeley Puma engines being substituted for the 360hp Rolls-Royce Eagles which were not available. The engines were pusher-puller pairs mounted in two nacelles. It first flew on August 13, 1918. Imperial War Museum, London

Braemar Mk.I

F. P. Rayham flew the first test flight of the Braemar Mk.I, as it had been named, on August 13, 1918. Acceptance trials were held on September 13 at Martlesham Heath. A series of tests proved that while performance and handling characteristics were good—it had achieved a top speed of 106mph with a gross load of 16,200lb—the pilot's controls and field of vision left a lot to be desired. Severe vibrations during taxi tests were encountered. Tie-rod breakages (a problem which this vibration may have contributed to) were experienced, but it was felt the bracing of the top and bottom wings to the center wing seemed to be equally responsible. The Braemar Mk.I was then sent to Farnborough where it remained until dismantled in 1920.

Braemar Mk.II

Most of these problems were corrected in the Mk.II, and 400hp Liberty engines replaced the Pumas. Cyril Uwins piloted the first flight on February 18, 1919, and found that the speed and rate of climb under a full load was better than anticipated. It was then flown to Martlesham Heath on April 17 and based there until the following February. Plans to convert it to a torpedo plane were being considered until November 1921 when it swung off the runway during a takeoff, hit one of the hangars, and was destroyed.

Pullman

It was decided the third prototype should be completed, but as a civil passenger aircraft capable of carrying fourteen passengers. It was renamed the Pullman, and made its maiden flight in May of 1920.

The Braemar Mk.II used the American Liberty 400hp engines since the Rolls still were unavailable. It was first flown on February 18, 1919, and performed well. However, it was wrecked during a takeoff when it swerved and hit a hangar at Martlesham Heath. Note the tandem-wheel narrow-track undercarriage. Bowers Collection

Put on exhibit at the International Aero Show at the Olympia exposition facility in July, it created a furor because of its size and cabin furnishings. Like the others it went on to Martlesham Heath but no attempt was ever made to fly it commercially, since the service pilots simply did not like it.

Tramps

During the period in which the Braemars were being tested, Captain Barnwell conceived a flying boat design based on the Braemar to be driven by a unit of four gasoline engines that later would be replaced by a steam-powered turbine of equivalent power. Initially Reid laid out a Pullman design capable of carrying fifty passengers, which he later reduced to forty and recommended that Maj. W. F. Vernon design a flying boat based on the Pullman design. In July the forty-passenger plane was dropped, but a contract was signed to design and build two prototypes to be called the Tramp. Consideration was given to a Tramp boat, but never got beyond the proposal stage. The two Tramps were built and completed in 1921 but never flew because of the transmission problems with the steam turbines. They were transported to Farnborough for development and experimentation by the Royal Aircraft Establishment (RAE).

Caproni Triplanes

Ca.40

The Italian Caproni Ca.40 series was a triplane development of the famous Ca.30 series of twin-fuselage trimotor bombers. As such, they were the only multimotored triplanes to be put into significant production during or after the war.

The configuration common to both the biplane and triplane was relatively unconventional. Both had an engine mounted in the nose of each fuselage and a pusher-type third engine at the rear of the central pod or nacelle that housed the crew, military load, and part of the defensive armament. The horizontal tail bridged both fuselages and extended well outboard of them. Three rudders without vertical fins were mounted on top of the stabilizer inline with the fuselages and the nacelle, sometimes called a Car or Gondola.

As a catch-all, the designation Ca.40 was used in reference to all of the big Caproni triplane bombers through the Ca.43 series, but there was another in the Ca.50 series. Although built for war use, some Ca.40s were modified for postwar use under later designations, and are described in chapter 6.

The Ca.40 was much more than just a Ca.33 with an added wing for more lift. It was much larger, with a wingspan of 98ft 1in (29.9m) compared to 76.75ft (23.4m) for the Ca.33. Wing area was 2,222sq-ft (206.2sq-m), compared to the 1,420sq-ft (131.8sq-m) of

The giant Caproni Ca.40 with its long, flat-sided nacelle and nose-wheel installation and eight-wheeled landing gear trucks. Courtesy F. Gordon Swanborough

the Ca.33. And there were five bays of struts on the wings outboard of the fuselages, instead of three. This led to the joke, meant for all aircraft with myriad struts and wires: "As a final rigging check, a bird was placed between the wings and if it flew out, a wire was missing!"

The fuselage-wing relationship of the Ca.40 differed notably from the Ca.30. On the latter, the fuselages and nacelle were mounted on the lower wing. On the Ca.40 they were attached to the underside of the center wing. Bombs were carried in a separate structure on the lower wing. On early versions this was a narrow box, with some of the bombs carried internally while others were hung on the outer sides of the wings. Later, the bombs were all carried internally in a much neater and streamlined housing. Engines varied from 250hp inlines, to straight-eights and V-12s up to 400hp.

Three Ca.40s were built in 1916. Information on engine installations is contradictory, but a reliable source quotes two 300hp engines in the fuselage and a 400hp engine in the nacelle. Another source lists the powerplants as three Isotta-Fraschinis of 200hp each or 270hp each.

The nacelle was flat sided and open on the top, with two pilots seated side by side. There was a gunner's position in the nose of the nacelle and another (two) in the cockpits in each fuselage located behind the wings. A pair of nose wheels were mounted under the nacelle and while these were supposed to be steerable, once the tail skids touched down they would have been of no value. They were probably more useful for protection against a nose-over of the top-heavy (20ft

high) monster. The undercarriage consisted of two eight-wheel bogies mounted under each fuselage. Length of the Ca.40 was 43ft (13.1m) and the gross weight was 14,300lb (6,470.6kg). With a top speed of only 78mph (125.6km/h), too slow for even a night bomber, the Ca.40 was discontinued in favor of an improved model.

Ca.41

To improve the performance of the Ca.40 the nacelle was extensively revised. On the Ca.41 this structure was shorter and narrower, with a rounded cross section and an enclosed top. The nose wheels were deleted and the two pilots now sat in separate tandem cockpits with the forward pilot doubling as the nose gunner. The high-drag vertical column radiator mounted on the Ca.40 fuselage was retained, and dimensions and weights stayed the same as for the Ca.40 although top speed now was increased to 84.5mph (136.1km/h).

The Ca.41 went into production in 1917. One example was sent to the United States after it entered the war because production of the design was being considered. The Ca.41 crashed on December 1, 1917, during a test flight. No Ca.41s were built in the United States but two firms, Fisher and Standard, did build Americanized versions of the Ca.30 with American Liberty engines.

Ca.42

The major production version of the Ca.4 series with still further aerodynamic refinements, tried more powerful engines including the Fiat, Isotta-Fraschini, and Liberty in the 300–400hp range. Most notable

The Caproni Ca.41 with the shorter streamlined nacelle and minus the nose-wheel assembly. The Ca.40's vertical radiators were retained. Bowers Collection

A major refinement of the Caproni Ca.42 was the use of nose radiators for the side engines. The external bomb bay was on the lower wing. Martin Caiden Collection

Four of the six Caproni Ca.42s built for the British RNAS. Shown are an access ladder and a refined bomb bay design. National Archives

refinement was in the use of nose radiators on the forward engines. Gross weight was up to 17,700lb (8,009.0kg), and top speed with the Liberty-powered version was 98mph (157.8km/h). The Ca.42 was flown by 181a and 182a Squadriglia. Separate production figures were not available, but between them thirty-five Ca.41s and Ca.42s were manufactured.

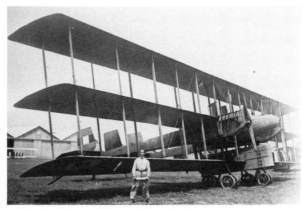

Closeup of the Ca.42 showing the bomb rack container. The figure on the nacelle nose appears to be a cartoon of Charlie Chaplin, the late film comedian. Interestingly, the wheels are not covered but the propeller is. Serial number appears to be 5375. Alberto Casirati Collection

The Ca.42 with the Charlie Chaplin cartoon on the nacelle nose. Notice the skid on the lower wing tip. Alberto Casirati Collection

The Caproni Ca.43 was a twin-float seaplane version of the Ca.42. The tail skids have not been removed, despite the floats. Bowers Collection

Ca.43

The seaplane version of the Ca.42 was tested by the Italian Navy under the new model designation Ca.43. A structural oddity was the shock-absorbing mounting for the twin floats. The military load was two standard naval torpedoes. Gross weight was 17,460lb (7,900.5kg), top speed 81mph (130.4km/h). No record of any production, however.

Ca.51

The Ca.51 was a single development of the Ca.42, with three 675hp Fiat A-14 V-12 engines. Other than large, circular nose radiators, the most notable change was to a biplane horizontal tail with six rudders

The single Caproni Ca.51 was a heavier version of the Ca.42, with 675hp engines and a six-rudder biplane tail. Note the tail machine-gun nest. Bowers Collection

The single-engine two-seat Caproni Ca.53. You can see the divergence of inboard ends of flying wires and the charac- *teristic Caproni rudder without a vertical fin.* National Archives

installed between the upper and lower surfaces. An additional feature was a streamlined pod mounted on the lower stabilizer for a tail gunner.

Ca.53

The Ca.53 was a single-engine two-seat triplane of conventional single-fuselage design built late in 1917. It was intended as a general-purpose military type and had provision for eight internally housed bombs. Only one was produced.

The Ca.53's span was 46ft 10in (14.3m), wing area 700sq-ft (65.0sq-m), gross weight 5,280lb (2,389.1kg), top speed 105–115mph (169.1–185.2km/h) depending on the particular Isotta-Fraschini engine installed. Power ranged from 350 to 500hp.

Curtiss Triplanes

The Curtiss alphabetical model designation system ended with the X-1 triplane early in 1917. After that, various letter or numerical designations were used. Some were entirely logical, as the model FL was

View of the Ca.53 shows the four-bladed propeller, the size of struts, and the overall clean but sturdy look of the triplane. National Archives

Ca.53 under restoration in Italy. You can see patches on both the lower and center wing, and on the fuselage. Alberto Casirati Collection

Closeup of the engine area on the Ca.53, showing the cooling vent arrangements. Alberto Casirati Collection

a combination of the existing F and L models. Other designations were rather capricious, such as using a friend's initials.

The era of cut-and-try model development at Curtiss had ended by mid-1917, after some nine larger triplanes had been developed in less than two years. Some of these reached production status, with one still to come from a different Curtiss company.

Once the United States had entered the war the emphasis was placed on production; furthermore, big business (mostly the auto industry) pretty well took over the small aviation industry. The new crop of executives at Curtiss knew little or nothing about airplane design or construction; in their minds, airplanes were going to be mass-produced like automobiles. Experimentation was discouraged at the government level. In addition to its established flying boat and trainer production, the Curtiss company now

was to turn out thousands of proven British aircraft like the S.E.5 single-seat and Bristol F.2B two-seat fighters.

The new order at Buffalo, New York, had no patience with a tinkerer like Glenn Curtiss and his cut-and-try methods. To get him out of the way, they put him in charge of a new branch of the company, Curtiss Engineering Corporation, located clear across the state at Garden City, a suburb of New York City. This experimental shop eventually built such low-priority projects as the Navy Curtiss flying boats that flew the Atlantic in 1919, and also produced the Model 18-T triplane fighter plane that briefly was the world's fastest airplane in 1918. The revolutionary Curtiss K-12 engine for the Model 18 was also developed at Garden City.

The Buffalo plant programs to build British designs were complete fiascos so Buffalo turned out only

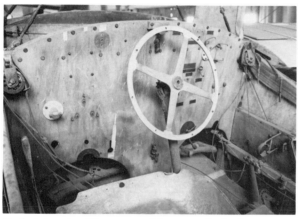

Cockpit interior. Placement of the control wheel appears to be offset to the right, although this is probably an illusion due to the camera angle. Alberto Casirati Collection

The aerial gunner's work area. The Scarff ring held a single machine gun that could be elevated, depressed, and swung through a wide arc for defensive protection. Alberto Casirati Collection

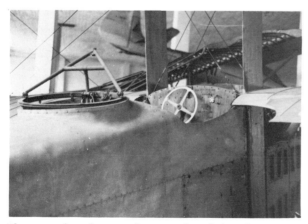

The gunner's cockpit in relation to the pilot's cockpit. In this photo, the control wheel is properly centered. Alberto Casirati Collection

The Ca.53 rudder mounting was sort of a Caproni trademark, as usual without any fin area. The original fabric seems to have held up well through the years. Alberto Casirati Collection

The Curtiss Autoplane of 1916 had Model L triplane wings fitted to an automobile body. Wings and tail were easily removed for use on the road. Bowers Collection

flying boats, biplanes, trainers, and a few big two-seat R-models that had been designed in 1915.

The larger Curtiss triplane designs from 1915 through 1918 are listed here by their alphabetical designation or name regardless of chronology, with the numbered Model 18 last.

Autoplane

The autoplane was a real tinkerer's dream—a flying automobile or, if you prefer, a roadable airplane. It was developed quickly for the Pan-American Aeronautical Exposition to be held in New York City in

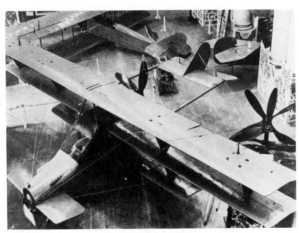

Overhead view of the Autoplane showing the nose and tail configuration and triplane wings to good advantage. Bowers Collection

February 1917. The "fuselage" was a complete three-seat automobile with an aluminum frame and body. This carried a 100hp Curtiss OXX-3 engine in the standard automobile location. An extension shaft to the rear drove a transmission to the rear wheels of the ground vehicle and turned a pulley that drove a four-bladed pusher propeller at the top of the cabin through a belt. The tail surfaces were supported on two wire-braced booms in the old Curtiss pusher tradition, and the wings were simply a set of Model L triplane wings adapted to fit.

The wings and tail were removable to allow the automobile unit to operate as a separate ground vehicle. The Autoplane, which was not known by any other designation, reportedly made a few straight-ahead hops before the show, but no further development was undertaken.

Model BT

The BT Flying Lifeboat, Model BT, of early 1917—there is no known significance to its designation letters—was another Glenn Curtiss brainstorm. It evolved from conversations between Curtiss and US Coast Guard officers concerning the need for a flying lifeboat. While the seaplanes of that time could land on fairly rough seas, they often were unable to take off again. Curtiss' idea was to have a hull of a flying boat double as a stout seaworthy lifeboat, with a self-contained powerplant that also drove the airplane propellers. If the seaplane was unable to take off in the rough sea, the wings and tail could be jettisoned and

Original form of the Curtiss BT-1 Flying Lifeboat, with the engine in the hull driving two oppositely rotating outboard propellers. National Air and Space Museum

FLYING LIFEBOAT
CRUISING AFTER SHEDDING WINGS.
MODEL B-T1

Artist's conception of the Curtiss BT after shedding its wings and tail at sea and proceeding purely as a boat, with its engine driving a marine propeller. Bowers Collection

the boat portion could then proceed under its own power.

To achieve this goal, Curtiss designed a short hull with a 200hp Curtiss V-2-3 engine installed in it to drive two propellers located on the middle wing of the triplane, set through shafts and gears. The tail surfaces were carried on booms.

The BT never flew in that configuration as the powerplant system was totally unworkable. With the war now on, the US Navy bought the BT, assigning Navy serial number A-2277, and had it converted to a more conventional single-propeller triplane with the engine mounted on the center wing driving the tractor propeller directly. In this form it was finally scrapped

on June 9, 1919. Span was 57ft (17.4m), length 40ft (12.2m), and height 16ft (4.9m).

Model FL

The Flying Boat, the one-only Model FL of early 1917, is a prime example of Curtiss methods of developing new models almost instantaneously. Major components of two existing models were combined to create a new design. In this case, the wings of the Model L triplane were fitted to the hull, tail, and engine of the Model F flying boat to make the Model FL. With a 100hp Curtiss OXX-3 engine, the FL was sold to the American Transoceanic Corporation before the United States entered the war and was advertised for sale by that firm in September 1919 for $6,000.

Judson Flying Boat

The Judson Flying Boat was another Curtiss design, and proof that not every Curtiss airplane got a model designation. This was especially true of designs built to the special order of a private individual. Such was the case of the triplane pusher flying boat built for a Mr. Judson. It appears in the Curtiss records only as the Judson Flying Boat. Built late in 1916 or early 1917, the Judson was essentially an enlarged Model F with three wide-chord wings braced by three bays of struts and powered by a 100hp Curtiss OXX engine. It remained in civilian hands during the war and was refitted with a 400hp Curtiss K-12 engine after the war. Later, it was used for exploration work in South America.

Final form of the Curtiss BT after purchase by the US Navy. The Navy redesigned the triplane to use a wing-mounted engine and a single direct-drive propeller. National Air and Space Museum

The Curtiss FL was a new model created by mating the wings of the L-1 triplane to the hull, tail, and engine of the Model F flying boat. Bowers Collection

80

The Curtiss Judson Flying Boat did not have a regular Curtiss model number, but was named after the person to whose special order it was designed and built. John Underwood Collection

The two-seat Curtiss Model L triplane of January 1917. Note the side-by-side seating, the discontinuity of the center wing across the fuselage, and the K-struts. Bowers Collection

Model L Series

The Model L triplane was a late 1916 design with an out-of-sequence model designation. Curtiss Models M, N, and O had been built in 1914, and the Model T was started in 1915.

The Model L was a two-seat triplane trainer that departed from the norm in two ways. First, the seating was side by side, as personally preferred by Glenn Curtiss. And second, the rear fuselage ended in a horizontal rather than a vertical knife-edge, a logical move in view of the extra width of the fuselage. The wings were unique in having a very narrow chord for a relatively long span. The closeness of the spars made the traditional strut and cross-wire arrangement difficult, so Curtiss developed an unusual rigid structure consisting of a vertical front strut and two crossing diagonal struts that formed a narrow letter X. This arrangement was adopted later for some of Curtiss' other narrow-wing triplanes. Sometimes the entire unit was enclosed in fabric; in others, only the forward gaps were covered.

The shortness of the lower wing raised a question of type designation. If an airplane like the French Nieuport 17, which had a narrow lower wing with only half the area of the upper, was called a sesquiplane (one and one half plane), what should a three-wing plane with a lower wing half the area of either of the other two be called?

The Model L series was the only one of the larger Curtiss wartime triplanes to attain a production status.

The original civilian two-seater had the 90hp Curtiss OX engine behind a circular radiator. A unique feature of the wing bracing wire system was that wires connecting the upper and lower wings passed through the center wing.

The Model L-1 was an improved version of the Model L but with slightly longer-chord wings and the gap increased by lowering the bottom wing and raising the upper. Only the forward gaps of the wing struts were covered. The engine appears to have been a 100hp OXX model.

Although not designed as a military airplane, the US Army bought one L-1 and assigned Army serial number 473 when it bought up many existing civil aircraft for use as trainers.

L-2 was a single-float seaplane version of the L-1 model. Three were ordered by the US Navy, with 100hp OXX engines and Navy serial numbers A-291–293. Originally the lower wing was as short as that on the L and L-1 models, but the span was increased to match the other two in order to carry the added weight of the float. The US Army acquired one of the several L-2s built, assigning it the Army serial number 475.

Model T

The Curtiss Model T Giant Flying Boat was a notable airplane in many respects. It was the first four-engine airplane in America, and was briefly the world's largest seaplane. It also featured the first power-boosted airplane control system in the world.

The Model T was designed to a British Air Ministry requirement, and an order was placed for twenty, with RNAS serial numbers 3073–3092.

The first Model T was assembled in the Buffalo factory in 1916, but it was without engines. The new

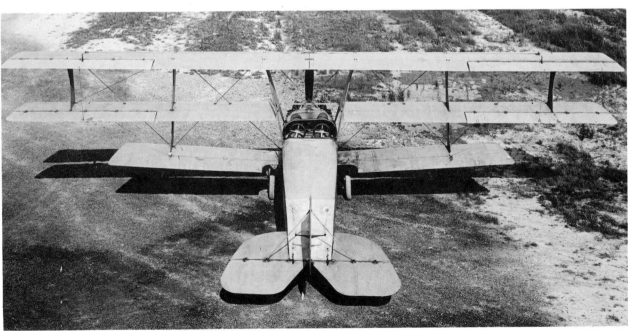

Rear view of the Curtiss L shows the side-by-side seating with dual-wheel controls, ailerons on the upper two wings only, *and the horizontal rather than the usual vertical knife-edge rear end of the fuselage.* Bowers Collection

200hp Curtiss V-4 engines to power it were not ready yet, so the Model T was shipped to England sans engines where four 240hp French Renault engines were installed with a novel feature: the two right-side engines rotated clockwise when viewed from the rear, and the two left-side engines rotated counterclockwise

The Curtiss Model L-1 was an enlarged and refined Model L. The short-span lower wing was now mounted below the *fuselage and was not continuous through the landing gear.* Bowers Collection

The Curtiss Model L-2s built for the Navy in 1917 originally had short lower wings like the earlier L models, but increased *the span to obtain extra lifting area to support the added weight of the floats.* Bowers Collection

to overcome trim problems resulting from engine torque. Because of the ongoing Wright brothers patent suit against Curtiss, the ailerons operated independently instead of together, with the active aileron moving to the down position. In light of later aeronautical knowledge, it would have been better to add its drag to the inside of the turn rather than the outside. Clumsy and underpowered, the Model T was not put into service and the remaining nineteen on order were canceled.

The Curtiss Model T, here being reassembled in England and fitted with French engines, was the first four-engine airplane built in the United States and for a brief time was the world's largest flying boat. J. W. Bruce Collection

Specifications:

Span, top wing 134ft (40.9m), middle 100ft (30.5m), bottom 78ft 4in (23.9m); length 58ft 10in (17.9m); height 31ft 4in (9.6m); wing area 2,812sq-ft (261.0sq-m); empty weight 15,645lb (7,079.2kg); gross weight 22,000lb (9,954.8kg); top speed 100mph (161km/h); rate of climb to 4,000ft (1,219.5m) 10min; endurance seven hours.

Model X-1

The X-1 trainer was the final model in the Curtiss alphabetical designation system. It was a two-seat tandem trainer of early 1917. This was apparently an attempt by Curtiss to produce a triplane trainer that did not have the side-by-side seating that the Army did not like in the Model L. The Model X-1 was, in effect, a Curtiss JN-4B fuselage, tail, and 90hp Curtiss OX engine fitted with the improved triplane wings of the Model L-1.

The Army did buy the X-1, but not with production in mind. After the United States got into the war they bought up a number of existing civil models for use as trainers. The X-1 received Army serial number 474.

Models 18-T and 18-B

By spring of 1918, the United States gave up on its idea of having the US aircraft industry build only proven foreign designs for its high-performance air-

The Curtiss Model X-1 trainer was essentially the tandem-seat Curtiss Model JN-4B fuselage and tail fitted with the wings and nose of the Model L-1 triplane. Bowers Collection

planes. American companies were given the green light to develop original combat airplanes.

The Curtiss Engineering Corporation at Garden City was quick to respond. The plant produced a fast two-seat fighter, the Model 18-T and the 18-B, both designed by Charles Kirkham. The T was the triplane, while the B was a biplane version. They also produced the revolutionary 400hp water-cooled and geared V-12 engine to power them. The Model 18s had absolutely no effect on later aircraft designs, but the compact and powerful Kirkham K-12 engine went on to become one of the world's most significant engines. Redesignated CD-12 (C for Curtiss and D for direct-drive), later simply D-12, it powered many US and foreign military airplanes into the early 1930s and set world speed records in racing planes. Enlarged as the Curtiss V-1570 Conqueror, it served the US Army up to 1940.

The Models 18-T and 18-B, named Wasp and Hornet by Curtiss, had a sleek semimonocoque fuselage with three layers of thin wood veneer formed in halves over a male mold and joined over a framework of stringers and bulkheads. For armament, the pilot was furnished with a pair of .30cal Marlin machine guns synchronized to fire through the propellers' arc while the gunner/observer had a pair of .30cal Lewis guns on a Scarff ring around the rear cockpit. For defense against attacks from below, he also had a single Lewis gun that fired through a port in the belly.

Model 18-T-1, the first of the two 18-Ts, built on a US Navy contract with Navy serial numbers A-7725 and A-7726, was completed with straight wings that had no dihedral. After its first flight on July 1, 1918, A-7725 was found to be tail heavy and was returned to the shop to have five degrees of sweep-back added to

The first Curtiss Model 18-T triplane, Navy serial number A-3325, was originally fitted with straight wings. Note the side-mounted radiators on the fuselage between the center and bottom wings. Joseph Nieto Collection

Because of initial tail heaviness, the first Curtiss 18-T was modified to give the wings a five-degree sweep-back to move

the center of lift aft. The instrumentation was boom mounted on this test airplane. Bowers Collection

the wings to move the center of lift aft and more in line with the center of gravity. Although officially named Wasp, the 18-T was nicknamed "Whistling Benny" around Garden City because of the distinctive sound made by its wires during landings. In its modified form, the 18-T-1 was loaned to the US Army for testing. During the tests it turned in a top speed of 163mph (262.4km/h) with a full military load in August of 1918 to become the fastest airplane in the world, albeit briefly and unofficially. Two additional 18-T-1s were built for the US Army with Army serial numbers 40054 and 40059.

The -1 designation was an addition to identify the original wings with one set of struts to a side, after interchangeable two-bay wings became available for the long-wing 18-T-2 model.

Specifications:
Span 32ft (9.8m); length 23ft 4in (7.1m); wing area 288sq-ft (26.7sq-m); empty weight 1,380lb (624.4kg); gross weight 3,050lb (1,380.1kg); top speed 162mph (261.0km/h); rate of climb to 12,500ft (3,811.0m) 120min; endurance 5.9hr.

For high-altitude research, with Navy support, Curtiss built longer wings, with a span of 40ft 7.5in (12.4m), and an area of 400sq-ft (37.1sq-m) for the version of the 18-T known as the 18-T-2. Both sizes of wings were readily interchangeable. Gross weight increased to 3,572lb (1,616.3kg) and top speed dropped to 139mph (223.8km/h). For a projected combat version, armament was reduced to one fixed machine gun and one flexible Lewis gun. With its long wings, 18-T-2 A-3325 flown by Curtiss pilot Roland Rholfs, set a new world's absolute altitude record of 34,910ft (10,423.8m) on September 18, 1919. In the meantime an additional Model 18-T was built as an 18-T-2 for service in Bolivia, where it operated successfully from La Paz whose elevation is 13,500ft (4,115.9m).

After the Armistice the Navy had no further use for the Model 18-Ts as combat aircraft, but held on to them because of their speed. The surprising postwar racing career of the Navy 18-Ts are covered in chapter 6.

Euler Triplane
The string of wartime Euler triplanes started in 1916 with a design conforming to the German Air Force specification for an armed two-seater heavier than the current 160hp C-types.

Euler chose the new 220hp Mercedes D.IV, an aeronautical oddity in being a straight-eight design. This engine was geared down so that the 1400rpm engine was reduced to a propeller speed of only 910rpm. This required either a larger-diameter propeller with wide blades or a normal-size four-blade type. Euler elected to use the four-blade version,

The long-span two-bay wings installed on the Curtiss 18-T A-3325. It was given the designation 18-T-2, and the original short-wing models became 18-T-1 to identify their one-bay wings. Bowers Collection

which rotated counterclockwise (left-handed) because of the gearing.

The airplane itself departed from the standard C-type not only by being a triplane, but by using side-by-side seating. The wider fuselage resulted in a different landing gear configuration. The forward struts ran straight down from the lower longerons instead of being splayed out. Because of the greater weight of the triplane, two wheels from lighter models were on each end of the axle.

The Euler did not win a production order nor an official designation. Various historians have called it a C-III or a DR.IV for historical convenience, but neither designation is correct.

Specifications:
Span 32ft 9.75in (10.0m); length 26.25ft (8.0m); wing area 405sq-ft (37.6sq-m).

Felixstowe Fury Triplane Flying Boat
Squadron Comdr. J. C. Porte, had visited the Curtiss plant in America and was impressed with their flying boat. Since he had helped develop the earlier Curtiss H and British F-series twin-engine flying boats, his plans to develop a greater giant flying boat finally were pressed forward under Contract A.S.17861 in mid-1918 to build a single example listed as the

Felixstowe P.S.B. (Five Eagle VIII), a terse description that implied that the aircraft was to be powered by five Rolls-Royce engines but did not mention that it was to be a triplane. Officially it was named the Fury; unofficially, it was named the Porte Super Baby. In June of 1918 a model of the hull was tested in the National Froude tank and the report was submitted in September. It was cleared for experimental flying on October

The Euler two-seat triplane of 1916, with the 220hp Mercedes eight-cylinder engine driving a left-handed four-bladed propeller. The vertical forward landing gear struts were attached to the extra-wide fuselage. Egon Kruger Collection

The Felixstowe Fury (unofficially known as Porte Super Baby) was designed by Squadron Comdr. J. C. Porte. Construction commenced in mid-1918 on a single aircraft using five Rolls-Royce Eagle VIII engines. It was a large triplane flying boat. RCAF

31. After testing, a new tail unit was designed and experimental turning indicators were installed. A second Fury was ordered and numbered N130, the original was numbered N123.

After the new tail structure was fitted, the Fury was flown by Porte and several other flying-boat veteran pilots. In 1919, plans were to made to ship it to Newfoundland for an attempt at a west-to-east flight across the Atlantic Ocean, but the flight by Alcock and Brown doomed the project. Later that year the Fury stalled during a landing, caving in the bottom and wrecking the plane. Work on the second Fury was stopped at once, ending Porte's designs at Felixstowe.

Specifications:

Powerplants, five Rolls-Royce VIII engines, two pairs mounted in tandem driving two double-blade tractor and two four-blade pusher propellers with the fifth pusher mounted between the others; span 123ft (37.5m); length 63ft (19.2m); wing area 3,108sq-ft (288.4sq-m); gross weight 25.3lb (11.4kg); top speed 97mph (156.2km/h).

Friedrichshafen FF-60 Triplane

The Flugzeugbau Friedrichshafen GmbH of Manzell, near Friedrichshafen, Germany, was the major producer of seaplanes for the German Navy but also manufactured twin-engine pusher land-based bombers for the Army. Its most extreme design effort resulted in the four-engine FF-60 of late 1918, a twin-float triplane intended for North Sea patrol and torpedo bombing operations.

Four 160hp Mercedes D.III engines were grouped close to the centerline in separate nacelles to reduce directional control problems under asymmetric power conditions. The biplane tail had four fins and rudders. The forest of float struts was characteristic of many German seaplane designs, but the twin floats

The Felixstowe Fury undergoing water-taxiing trials in September of 1918. Note that the left outboard rear engine has not been started while the two nose propellers are running; the other two rear props are apparently just being started. This is another of Porte's designs based on the Curtiss three-engine flying boat. RCAF

The Fury with its newer tail structure was flown by Porte during the testing that started on October 31, 1918. In 1919 it was going to be shipped to Newfoundland to make a west-to-east crossing of the Atlantic, but Alcock and Brown's successful flight in the Vimy scuttled the effort. RCAF

The FF-60 taking off on a test flight. The close spacing of the engines was to minimize directional trim problems should it be necessary to shut down an engine. Notice the large number of struts on the floats and the center section bracings. Alex Imrie Collection

As large as the FF-60 was, the German Navy had a crane strong enough to lift it in or out of the water and then move it in either direction on an overhead rail-beam with precision control by the crane operator. Bowers Collection

were separately mounted to provide space that enabled bombs or torpedos to be dropped freely between the floats.

Three FF-60s were ordered by the German Navy, serials 3301–3303, but apparently only one was delivered. The fate of the other two is not known.

LaBourdette-Halbron Triplane Flying Boat

The outstanding feature of the 1918 LaBourdette-Halbron triplane was the twin-hull configuration, one of only two produced during World War I and one of the very few in all of aviation history. This French design was meant to be a torpedo plane, but its stability in the water due to the two full-sized hulls was more than offset by the weight of the hulls and the strain imposed on the interconnecting structure by unsymmetrical water loads during takeoffs and landings as well as while taxiing.

The pilot and rear gunner were positioned in the central nacelle mounted on the center section of the

Mechanics installing one of the Hispano-Suiza engines on the LaBourdette-Halbron torpedo triplanes. The rearward stagger of the wings does not show up in this photo. Bowers Collection

The LaBourdette-Halbron being readied for launching. The twin hulls and twin rudders can be seen as well as the pilot's and rear gunner's pod. The ailerons were on the top and center wing only. Note the strut arrangements and tie-rod braces that held the rear of the hulls together. Bowers Collection

The Levy-Besson triplane number 68 being launched into the River Seine during water taxiing trials. It had a 150hp Renault pusher-type engine. Heinz J. Nowarra Collection

bottom wing, and there was a gunner's station in the bow of each hull. The wings had a considerable negative stagger. It was powered by two 200hp Hispano-Suiza pusher engines that were mounted on the middle wing.

Wing are was 1,076sq-ft (99.9sq-m), and gross weight was 7,040lb (3,185.5kg). Only two were produced.

Levy-Besson Triplane Flying Boat

Marcel Besson specialized in designing triplane flying boats. His first effort in 1915 was a small triplane with a 95hp engine. It was not successful because it was underpowered, but the design was a sound one. Having no manufacturing resources, all of his designs were produced by George Levy, a financier who also owned an aircraft factory. Levy would eventually build Besson's designs in series.

By 1916, Besson had produced another triplane design featuring a unique wing arrangement. The top and lower wings were of equal span, but the center wing had at least 33 percent more wingspan and area. The engine was located between a pair of struts that joined the upper wing to the hull; the engine mounting was braced by diagonal struts to ensure that the engine was firmly secured. The larger engine produced 150hp.

The wings were single-bay types. Though it was successful, it did not go into production.

In keeping with the tradition of designing a new model every year, Besson, in 1917, produced a triplane fighter flying boat. It was powered first by a Hispano-Suiza 180hp engine, and later by a 200hp Hispano. It used an I-form interplane strut with ailerons on the top and middle wings. While it was similar to the 1916 model, the center wingspan was reduced and did not protrude as far. A more stable mounting was installed on the 200hp version, and a cooling radiator was mounted on the center wing. The Georges Levy company built over one hundred of this type to be used on coastal patrols and for antisubmarine activities.

The next year, 1918, Besson brought out another triplane flying boat powered by a 450hp engine that was capable of carrying a payload of 4,400lb (1,991.0kg). Later, the design was adapted to accommodate three 350hp Lorraine engines. Since it was designed to have a range of 1,120mi (1,803.2km) and this feature found favor with the French Navy who wanted a long-range patrol flying boat to use in the Mediterranean and Atlantic areas, an order for 200 was placed in 1917.

The triplane had folding wings, another unusual feature for a triplane. A sixty-gallon fuel capacity permitted an endurance of four hours, sufficient for a

Number 68's engine mounting and sleek hull with single step. The two cockpits were placed forward of the wings for better field of vision. US Navy

long patrol sortie. Since the pilot and observer cockpits were well forward they had a wide field of view, and a cutaway in the hull gave an excellent downward view. The latter, though, had its drawbacks because it meant that tight-fitting canvas covers were needed when the plane was moored to keep seawater from coming into the hull in rough water. The hull was made of cedar plywood. The three motors were mounted on the center wing, one as a pusher and the other two as tractors. The tail surfaces were strongly braced since the rear of the hull was thin and narrow.

Lloyd Triplane Bomber

In 1916 the Ungarische Lloyd Flugzeug und Motorenfabrik Aszod produced an experimental triplane bomber known only as the 40.08, which was its military serial number. Lloyd had been manufacturing biplane reconnaissance aircraft since 1914 and the first version, the C-I, had set an altitude record of over 20,000ft (6,098m). The 40.08 was their first attempt at designing a bomber.

Generally similar to the Italian Capronis, the 40.08 had twin fuselages and a center nacelle. Crew stations were provided in both fuselages as well as the nacelle. Each fuselage had a nose-mounted 200hp Austro-Daimler tractor engine, with a 360hp Austro-Daimler pusher engine mounted in the nacelle. The aircraft was an all-wooden design with the fuselages and large wing areas covered by plywood. Fuselages

and nacelle were mounted on the center wing. Landing gear consisted of two sets of wheels mounted underneath the fuselages on each side. The strut arrangement consisted of two bays slanted inward between the top and center wings, but only a single bay of struts also slanted inward between the shorter bottom wing and the center wing.

It was a strange, ungainly looking airplane. Unfortunately it crashed and was destroyed on its first flight, so no performance figures are available. The design was dropped.

LVG G-III Triplane

The LVG-III was designed and built by Luft Verkehrs Gesellschaft in 1918 at Johannisthal Aerodrome, in Germany. LVG was one of the largest, if not the largest, aircraft works. It was assembled in the Parseval airship sheds. The LVG name translates as the Aeronautical Transport Company, or earlier the Air Traffic Company Limited which ran the airship company using the Parseval airships.

Following the lead of Gotha and Friedrichschafen large bombers, the four-seat LVG G-III featured the tractor engine style. It did retain the traditional nose-gun position that Gotha and Friedrichschafen had elected to delete. A right-hand propeller on the starboard engine was opposed by a left-hand propeller on the port engine. This was to be a torque-balancing measure. The fuselage was a semimonocoque struc-

The Lloyd 40.08 was a bomber built by Ungarische Lloyd Flugzeug und Motorenfabrik Aszod in 1916. The fuselage-powerplant arrangement was similar to the Italian Capronis, but crew members rode in both fuselages and the nacelle. A

single 360hp Austro-Daimler engine was mounted as a pusher in the nacelle while a pair of 200hp Austro-Daimlers were mounted in the fuselage noses. It was an all-wooden aircraft that crashed on its first flight. Bowers Collection

Side view of the biplane tail and double rudders on the LVG G-III triplane. It had a swivel machine-gun mount in the nose gunner's station, and the radiators were mounted atop the engines. Alex Imrie Collection

Head-on photo of the LVG G-III showing the gap between the center wing, the bracing struts from the fuselage to the wings, and the wide undercarriage with the double sets of wheels. Ailerons were mounted on the top and bottom wings. Alex Imrie Collection

ture of laminated wood veneer, a departure from standard practice in the large German aircraft but which was common on the fighters. Only a single Type III was built by LVG but it had been their intention to license to Schutte-Lanz, and the plane would have been designated the Schul G-V. But it never reached the production stage by the time the war ended.

Specifications:

Powerplants, twin Maybach 260hp; span 80ft (24.4m); length 41ft (12.5m); wing area 1,238sq-ft (114.9sq-m); gross weight 9,000lb (4,073.4kg); top speed 81mph (50.2km/h).

Mannesmann (Poll) Triplane

This giant triplane seems to have been a dying gasp of the German Air Force. It was meant to carry leaflets across the Atlantic Ocean to drop on New York City. While the designer's name seems to be a bit of a mystery, it is believed that it was the work of Villehad Forssman who had worked previously for Siemens-Schuckert. The unfinished aircraft was discovered in a hangar after the Armistice by the Allied Control Commissions inspection team.

A section of the plane and a wheel 8ft in diameter were sent back to England for study. The span of the center wing was 165ft (50.3m); the top and bottom wings were of equal span, but quite a bit smaller. It was to have tandem-mounted engines, eight on the center wing and a pair on the lower wing. The fuselage was long and slender, mounted between the center wing directly above the engines on the lower wing. The fuselage was 150ft (45.7m) long.

An eighty-hour flight endurance was planned, and provision was made to carry such a load of fuel. The overall structure was very heavy, yet extremely weak. No internal bracing cable was installed, and while it was covered with two layers of three-ply wood, which made it as heavy as a boat, these did little to add strength. In addition the ailerons were too small, the center of gravity was way aft, and the elevators would have been ineffective. So it is doubtful that it would have flown if it had been completed.

Morane-Saulnier TRK Triplane

The Morane-Saulnier TRK triplane bomber was a departure from the Morane traditional designs in several ways. The fuselage was a semimonocoque structure of laminated wood veneer. It was powered by a pair of 230hp water-cooled Salmson radials mounted back to back in the fuselage driving tractor propellers by means of extension shafts and bevel gearing. The propellers rotated in opposite directions. It had two sets of two wheels each, plus a single wheel mounted under the nose to prevent nose-over damage on landings.

The Moranes of World War I used various combinations of letters for factory model designations. Those accepted for military use were given official numerical designations in sequence of the number of models, the best known being the Model XXII Parasol monoplane.

Nieuport and General Aircraft Company Triplane

The Nieuport London was designed in 1918 by Henry P. Folland who had designed the famous S.E.5 fighter. The London was a wooden-frame light bomber intended for night missions.

The company had been formed before the war to build French designs under license, but also built British designs and turned out a few original designs.

The Morane-Saulnier TRK was a large bomber whose size is emphasized by comparison to the men in the photo. The *propeller drive-shaft mountings are visible, as is the double landing gear.* Bowers Collection

The London initially was to have been powered by ABC radials, but the Dragonfly Mk.I was not yet available when the prototype was finished, so for the flight trials, 230hp Pumas were installed in the prototype, which was redesignated the Mk. II.

Specifications for the Mk.I were: span 59.5ft (18.1m); length 37.5ft (11.4m); wing area 1,100sq-ft (102.1sq-m); top speed 100mph (161km/h).

Six Londons were ordered but only two, serials H1740 and H1741, were built. The other four were canceled in November of 1918 before work on them had begun.

H1740 made its first flight on April 13, 1920, at Acton, England, and H1741 flew in July of 1920. A quarter-inch-thick match board with tongue and groove were used to cover the square-cut fuselage. The movable parts of the tail were about the only stream-lined part of the plane. The wings were equal in span and had two bays, were unstaggered, and equipped with six horn-balanced ailerons. After testing, the ailerons on the upper and center wing were deleted. The single-wheel divided landing gear was mounted beneath the wings and engines, and a pair of Lewis guns on a Scarff ring was installed in the nose cockpit. It was to have carried nine 250lb (113.1kg) bombs or an equivalent load of the same weight.

Packard-Le Pere LUSAO-11 Triplane

The Packard-Le Pere LUSAO-11 was a three-seat triplane designed by a Captain Le Pere on loan from the French government via their French Aviation Mission, and built in 1918 by the Packard Motor Car

View of the bevel gear and drive shaft as well as the propeller mounting on the TRK. The small, four-bladed propeller on the nose probably drove a generator. You can also see the twin side-by-side cockpits with their windscreens, radiator placement between the middle and top wings, and the auxiliary nose wheel. Bowers Collection

Company. It was to have been a high-altitude long-range surveillance plane. The L stood for Le Pere and the USAO for US Army Observation, under a briefly used system that existed from 1918–1920. The first prototype was delivered in February of 1919 and the second was delivered later in the year.

The planes were built with a laminated veneer fuselage and rigid wooden-box wing strut assemblies. Armament was to have been three Lewis guns and one 37mm cannon; an alternate was four .30cal machine guns. Two Liberty twelve-cylinder 400Ls of 425hp each furnished the power.

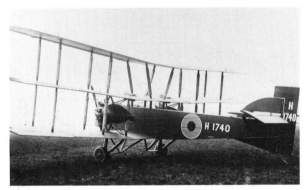

Serial number H1740 was the first Nieuport London to fly. Observe the undercarriage, angular tail surfaces, and streamlined engine mountings. Only two were built.

Specifications:

Span 54.5ft (16.6m); length 38ft 2in (11.6m); height 14ft (4.3m); wing area 870sq-ft (80.7sq-m); empty weight 5,455lb (2,468kg); gross weight 8,577lb (3,881kg); top speed 112mph (180.32km/h); cruising speed 94mph (151.34km/h); rate of climb to 6,500ft (1,981.7m) 9.3min; service ceiling 15,350ft (4,679.9m); maximum ceiling 17,300ft (5,274.4m); range at 106mph (170.7km/h) 475mi (764.8km).

Sopwith Triplanes

In addition to its three single-seat triplane fighters, Sopwith also produced larger two- and three-seat models and two versions of a twin-engine model.

LRT Tr

Although the Tripehound precedes the three-place Model LRT Tr in most listings of Sopwith triplanes, probably because of its great fame, the LRT Tr is obviously a considerably earlier design even though it flew at about the same time in 1916.

The LRT Tr was a three-seater and the designation is believed to mean Long Range Tractor Triplane. It was a fighting airplane, developed to the same requirements as the Armstrong-Whitworth F.K.12. Developed as a long-range escort for bombers or for defense against Zeppelin raiders, the big plane had a novel armament setup. Instead of a synchronized nose gun or a swivel-mounted flexible gun in the rearmost of the three open cockpits, the gunner was seated in a streamlined nacelle atop the upper wing. No details on the armament exist, but the use of an automatic cannon

This three-quarter view shows the double-wheel trucks and landing gear arrangement of the Packard-Le Pere LUSAO-11 triplane. Also shown are the three inverted V-strut arrange-ments over the fuselage and engines, and the clean motor housings. The middle wing is slightly shorter than the other two. Four-bladed propellers were fitted. USAF Museum

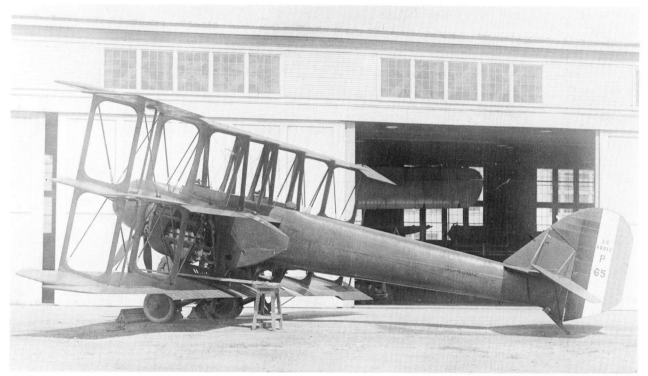

A three-quarter rear view of the LUSAO-11's cockpits, interplane struts, and streamlined rear motor nacelles. The rudder bears the designation S.C. 40012-P-65. USAAC via G. S. Williams

Profile shows the clean lines of the triplane's fuselage. Ailerons were mounted on all three wings. Note the sturdy interplane strut arrangement. USAAF

The three-seat Sopwith LRT Tr was a long-range escort fighter and anti-zeppelin airplane. It had unique four-wheel landing gear, wide struts, and a vertical fin. Bowers Collection

This view of the LRT Tr shows the streamlined teardrop gunner's position on the top wing, the strut arrangement, and the extended exhaust stack. Imperial War Museum, London

in the 20–30mm range has been suggested. Powerplant was a 250hp geared twelve-cylinder water-cooled Rolls-Royce Mk. II, an early model of the later famous Eagle.

The landing gear was another novelty for the time, a four-wheel unit on which the rear wheels were right under the airplane's center of gravity. The plane could then rest either on its nose wheels or on the tail skid. The nose wheels were a comfort to the gunner's peace of mind, as they prevented nose-overs in rough or soft ground situations that could be dangerous to him. The center wings were well above the upper longerons, but were closed off by a high fuselage superstructure. Because of the extremely narrow wings, the spar spacing would not allow use of traditional parallel interplane struts with crossed incidence wires. Instead, wide single struts were used as one-piece units that were continuous from the top to the bottom wing. Ailerons were fitted to all three wings. Because of the position of the struts, both the flying and landing wires passed through the center wing. Altogether the LRT Tr had more disadvantages than advantages, so only the prototype was built. Span was 53ft (16.2m), length was 38ft (11.6m).

2B-2 Rhino

The 2B-2 Rhino two-seater triplane differed from its predecessor Sopwith triplanes in having both a model designation, 2B-2 (for two-place bomber) and an assigned name Rhino.

Two Rhinos (RNAS serials X-8 and X-9) were built late in 1917 as bombers powered with the 230hp BHP (Beardmore-Halford-Pullinger) six-cylinder water-cooled engine. These did not follow the Hispano triplanes lead in using a neat nose radiator. Instead, a single honeycomb block was installed on each side of the nose. A new feature for a single-engine bomber of that era was the internal stowage of the bombs, four 112lb (50.7kg), nine 50lb (22.6kg), or ten to twenty 20lb

(9.1kg) were carried internally instead of on external racks under the belly or lower wing.

As on the Model LRT Tr triplane, the center wing roots were above the upper longerons, with the fuselage superstructure built up to cover the ends. The aerodynamic gain from this compared to the single-seat airplane was largely negative; however, by cutting two separate gaps in each center wing root they provided better downward visibility to both the pilot and gunner to a limited degree.

The use of triplane wings was a logical choice for getting the required wing area for heavy loads into a reasonable wingspan. Using a wide chord allowed for normally spaced spars, parallel interplane struts, and crossed wire rigging. Flying and landing wires were passed through the center wing. Horn-balanced ailerons, a first for Sopwith, were fitted to all three wings.

The two Rhinos differed notably in minor details. X-8 did have the horn-balanced ailerons, but differed in the rear cockpit armament installation. Both were tested in February and March of 1918, but did nothing

The second of the two Sopwith 2B-2 Rhino triplane bombers built early in 1918. This one, RNAS serial number X-9, is distinguishable from the first in that it does not have the horn-balanced ailerons. Frederick G. Freeman Collection

Although carrying the lowest RAF serial number of the three Sopwith Cobham bombers, H671 was designated as Mk. II because it was fitted with substitute Siddeley Puma water-cooled engines in lieu of the long-delayed ABC Dragonfly radial engines. Bowers Collection

The Sopwith Cobham designated Mk. I flew long after the Mk. II because of ABC engine delays. Compare the wing stagger and tail with the Mk. II. Bowers Collection

Front view of the Cobham Mk.I showing installation of the 360hp nine-cylinder air-cooled ABC Dragonfly radial engine. Landing gear configuration was unusual. Bowers Collection

to advance the art of single-engine bomber design and were soon retired.

Specifications:

Span 41ft (12.5m); length 30.25ft (9.2m); wing area 112sq-ft (10.4sq-m); empty weight 2,185lb (988.7kg); gross weight 3,590lb (1,624.4kg); top speed 103mph (165.8km/h).

Cobham

Named for the famous British pilot Alan Cobham (later Sir Alan), the Cobham was a three-seat, twin-engine bomber designed in the summer of 1918 to use 360hp ABC Dragonfly engines. Three prototypes, serials H671–673, were ordered. The fuselage structure was conventional, but the wings owed much to the Snark for their structure and strutting.

Because of delay problems with the ABC engines, H671 was fitted with a 240hp water-cooled Siddeley Puma engine and became the Cobham Mk.II. The uncompleted ABC versions then became the Mk.I.

Three-person crew in the cockpit of a Sperry amphibian triplane. The tail boom shows up well, along with the tail planes. The American cockades on the upper wing and rudder markings were applied in standard military positioning. The prototype was completed too late to see service in World War I. Fred C. Dickey, Jr., Collection

Low end-of-the-war priorities kept even the Mk. II from flying until mid-1919. The first Mk. I with a notably different vertical tail did not fly until March 1920. Official interest by that time was nil, and the wartime contract under which they were built was canceled.

Specifications:

Span 54ft (16.5m); length 38ft (11.6m); gross weight 6,300lb (2,850.7kg).

Sperry Amphibian Triplane

The Lawrence Sperry Aircraft Corporation of Farmingdale, Long Island, New York, designed and developed a pusher amphibian triplane as a light bomber. Unfortunately it was completed too late to be considered for wartime production. Its significance rests with it being the first serious attempt to build a practical amphibian using a retractable landing gear in a flying-boat-type hull. Another unconventional feature of this Sperry was its short hull and tail surfaces carried on booms in the fashion of early land pushers. The three man crew rode in a single cockpit. Because of the need to maintain a watertight hull, the bombs had to be carried on wing racks under each wing. This was Sperry's only attempt at building a triplane.

Specifications:

Powerplant, low-compression 330hp Liberty; span 48ft (14.6m); length 31.5ft (9.6m); wing area 678sq-ft (62.9sq-m); gross weight 7,044lb (3,187.3kg); top speed 85mph (136.9km/h).

Tarrant Tabor Triplane

The contract for the Tabor, as let by the RAE, specified a machine with a flight range capable of bombing Berlin from bases in Britain. Construction details had to be such that "indigenous timber" would

The Sperry, about to land, with its retractable gear, wing float, engine mounting, and strut arrangement. The bomb rack is positioned under the lower wing. The crew has close quarters in their single cockpit. US Navy

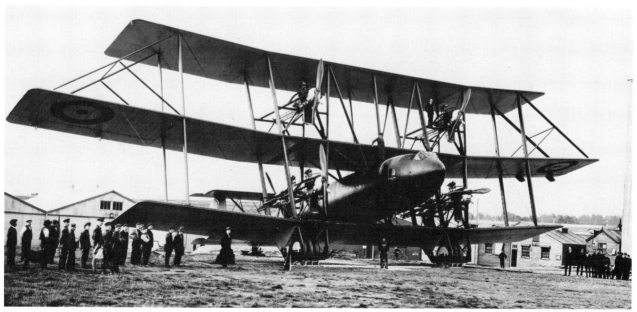

The Tarrant Tabor triplane just before the taxi tests, emphasizing the huge size of the airplane. Capt. F. G. Dunn is in civilian clothes standing next to the upper port engine. He was killed in a crash shortly after this photo was taken. Capt.

P. T. Rawlings also lost his life in the crash. Factory foreman Edney is standing on the fuselage and was aboard when the crash occurred, but was not injured. US Navy

be used and construction methods would allow for employing female labor. W. G. Tarrant, a building contractor from Surrey whose firm early in the war had become a subcontractor building wooden components for major airplane manufacturers, was awarded the contract. It called for two prototypes to be built simultaneously. Using the Warren girder technique, small wooden components were assembled to form strong, large-sized structural members. Since the Tarrant firm was inexperienced in metalworking, the RAE at Farnborough was to furnish the metal fittings, and build, cover, and flight test the planes.

Assembly was carried out in the C Balloon shed, and the finished plane was so large it had to be rolled out sideways when it was completed, using trolleys on rails. The Tabor's top wing was higher than the roof of a four-story building. It weighed 16,000lb (7,240kg) empty, and its 131ft (39.9m) wingspan was finally topped by the B-29 of World War II. Wing area totaled 5,000sq-ft (564sq-m). Originally designed to take four 600hp Siddeley Tiger engines, Tarrant had to settle for six 450hp Napier Lions because of problems with the Tiger engine, a common occurrence of the times. The two additional engines had to be mounted somewhere so they were placed higher up between the middle and top wings.

Finally completed after the war, as the RAE had also envisaged it as a commercial transport and allowed

work to go on to completion, it was ready for flight testing on May 26, 1919. Last-minute calculations seemed to indicate it might be tail heavy, so Tarrant ordered a half-ton of lead loaded into the nose. Since each propeller had to be hand swung to start it, it took up to an hour to get them started. Finally, with Capt. F. G. Dunn as first pilot and Capt. P. T. Rawlings as copilot, they taxied the Tabor back and forth on the field, trying the controls and making turns, when Dunn turned the plane ponderously into the wind to try a straight takeoff run. Opening up the lower engines, he got the tail off the ground and then opened up the top engines to get full takeoff power. The Tabor abruptly nosed over; the nose hit the ground, crumbling and splintering and gouging a deep furrow in the turf. The tail came up higher, and the front propellers began chewing up dirt. The undercarriage and wings dug in, and the Tabor went over on its back. When it came to rest, the tail was up in the air like a giant bomb.

Captains Dunn and Rawlings died as a result of injuries from the crash. There are conflicting stories of the casualties, however. One states that a Captain Wilson, a technical observer, also died in the crash, and that three RAE foremen had been passengers. Other reports state that Captain Wilson had been in the tail and escaped through a port hole in the rear, and that the other three got out safely. Thus it would seem that Dunn and Rawlings were the only fatalities, as they

The 1915 Voisin Triplane I bomber bears resemblance to the 1916 Triplane II model. It had the same twin-fuselage design, but the Triplane I fuselages were angular types while the Triplane II fuselages were round. The nose wheel also is quite different. The triangular cloth additions to the rudder of the

Triplane I were not applied on the 1916 model, nor were the outer upper cloth panels. And the 1915 model sits lower on its undercarriage. Joseph Frantz is standing by the cockpit. Courtesy Alain Pelletier

were thrown clear in the crash and the fuselage rolled over on them.

Specifications:

Powerplant, six Napier Lion engines of 500hp each; span, top wing 98ft 5in (30.0m), center wing 131.25ft (40.0m); bottom wing 98ft 5in (30.0m); length 73ft 2in (22.3m); height 37.25ft (11.4m); wing area 4,950sq-ft (459.4sq-m); body diameter 11ft (3.4m); wing gap between each wing 14.75ft (4.5m); chord gap 15ft 2in (4.6m); span of tail planes 30ft (9.2m); gap of tail planes 10ft (3.1m); gross weight with combat load 44,672lb (20,213.6kg).

As an item of interest, one of the designers on the project was Walter H. Barling who will be heard from again later in the book.

Voisin Triplanes

Gabriel Voisin, a pioneer French aviator and builder, designed a large experimental bomber in 1915. Triplane I was huge by the contemporary standards.

The fuselages were long and narrow and were placed one above the other; the top fuselage was smaller than the main one, but had a gunner's position in the nose. The fuselages were angular and the rudder was a half circular form. A very large nose wheel supplemented the main landing gear. It was powered by four 250hp Salmson A.9 engines mounted under the center wing in tandem pairs. The pilot sat in a cabin that was fully enclosed. The span was 125ft (38.1m).

In 1916 the pressing need was for a bomber capable of carrying a heavier bomb load over a greater distance—they had Berlin in mind. And even though Triplane I was abandoned, Voisin was given an order to study the problem and hopefully produce an aircraft that would meet the needs of the high command. It called for a plane able to carry twelve 220mm shells (bombs). Voisin claimed that it took only thirty-six days to have a design flying. Triplane II followed the format of Triplane I in being a twin-fuselage design, but the fuselages were round rather than angular and had two sets of dual wheels under the centerline, just ahead and behind the lower wing, with other dual pairs under the

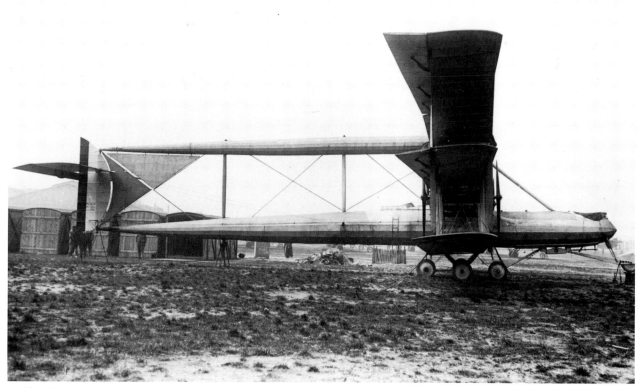

Profile of the Voisin Triplane I with its twin fuselages, cloth-covered outer upper struts to increase lift, the nose wheel, and unusual undercarriage. Bowers Collection

engines as stabilizing outriggers. The nose wheel of Triplane I was retained, but was smaller and had a cover over the upper portion of the wheel. The two outermost slanting struts between the middle and top wing were covered with cloth to provide added lift.

Specifications:
Powerplant, four 200hp Hispano-Suizas tandem-mounted on middle wing; span 118ft (36.0m); length 71.5ft (21.8m); wing area 2,152sq-ft (199.7sq-m); top speed 77.5mph (124.8km/h); gross weight 14,300lb (6,470.6kg).

This view of the Voisin highlights the fuselage construction, placement of the engines, nose-wheel covering, and strut arrangement. The upper outer struts are in a vee formation and the outer ones are cloth covered. The other struts are inclined inward on each wing. Bowers Collection

The cloth coverings of the outer upper struts have been removed and the small propeller on the nose of the upper fuselage shows clearly. The canvas closures on the wide hangar in the background were fairly common in lieu of doors. Bowers Collection

The radiators mounted on both front and back of the center wing. You can see the cloth-covered center struts between the fuselages. Bowers Collection

Yes, it did fly! The Voisin taking off with full crew aboard. Note how high the nose wheel is in relation to the main gear. It *seems obvious its main purpose was to prevent a nose-over from occurring during a bad landing.* Bowers Collection

Chapter 5

World War I Multiplanes

The military requirements of World War I pretty much standardized the general configuration of the airplane. Gone entirely were the freakish configurations, as well as the canards and most of the tandem-wing designs. Multiplane concepts were not entirely swept aside by the new standardization, but the majority developed during the war conformed to accepted standards and merely added extra wings to biplanes or triplanes. While four wings seemed to find the most favor with designers, there were exceptions.

Even so, a surprising number of multiplane prototypes were designed and built. Even more surprising is the fact that some actually achieved production

status—some of the single prototypes were put into military service.

Armstrong-Whitworth Quadruplanes
F.K.9

In the summer of 1916 Armstrong-Whitworth and Company, Limited designed as a private venture the F.K.9, a two-seat fighter-reconnaissance quadruplane. Initial tests were conducted, and indicated that a number of modifications were in order. As a result new wings with enlarged ailerons, a larger fin, a redesigned engine cowling, and an increased track were introduced. The revised F.K.9 was powered by a 110hp Clerget 9Z rotary engine and was officially tested

The Armstrong-Whitworth F.K.9 was a two-seat fighter-bomber that became the prototype of the production Model

F.K.10. The wing and strut arrangement resembled the Sopwith models. Bowers Collection

during November and December of 1916 at the Central Flying School. In addition a production contract was signed for fifty planes of an improved version, the F.K.10. Armament consisted of a fixed .303cal Vickers machine gun and a free .303cal Lewis gun on a flexible mount.

Specifications:

Empty weight 1,226lb (554.8kg); gross weight 2,038lb (922.2kg); top speed 94mph (151.3km/h) at 6,500ft (1,981.7m), 87mph (140.1km/h) at 10,000ft (3,048.8m); rate of climb to 6,500ft (1,981.7m) 14min 32sec; endurance 3hr.

F.K.10

Derived from the F.K.9 after undergoing major design changes, the F.K.10 two-seater reconnaissance quadruplane kept only the basic wing structure of the F.K.9. On December 30, 1916, the production contract was given to Angus Sanderson and Company of Newcastle-on-Tyne to produce the fifty airplanes, but after only five were manufactured, the contract was canceled. However, three more had been ordered for the RNAS, on separate contracts: two were to be produced by the Phoenix Dynamo Manufacturing Company and one from the Armstrong-Whitworth company. These three were eventually completed and tested. Armament was the same as for the F.K.9. While the 130hp Clerget was the standard engine, at least one was tested with a 110hp LeRhone rotary engine.

Specifications:

Span 27ft 10in (8.5m); length 22.25ft (6.8m); height 11.5ft (3.5m); wing area 390.4sq-ft (36.2sq-m); empty weight 1,236lb (559.3kg); gross weight 2,019lb (913.6kg); top speed 84mph (135.24km/h) at 6,500ft (1,981.7m), 74mph (119.1km/h) at 10,000ft (3,048.8m); rate of climb to 6,500ft (1,981.7m) 15min 50sec; endurance 2hr 30min.

The first F.K.10 built by Armstrong-Whitworth and fitted with a 110hp LeRhone engine. Compare fuselage and tail details with the F.K.9 prototype. Bowers Collection

The Euler quadruplane. Because the upper wing was pivoted to function as ailerons, the traditional flying and landing wires were installed between the second-from-top wing to the bottom wing. The gaps between the top three wings, and the one between the bottom and second wing, varied. Peter M. Grosz Collection

The single outer wing strut, rigging, and wing stagger on the Euler quadruplane. The second wing from the bottom restricts the pilot's downward view somewhat. Peter M. Grosz Collection

Euler Quadruplane

Since his design attempts at a biplane and triplane failed to produce an acceptable fighter, Julius Hromadnik, Euler's chief designer, hoped a new approach might offer a better chance of success so he decided to try his luck with a quadruplane. He used the fuselage, tail section, and 100hp Oberursel Ur.I engine of the experimental single-seat fighter unofficially referred to as the D.II, and simply fitted it with four wings.

Unlike most quadruplanes, this neat little fighter design had the two lower wings connected to the upper and lower fuselage longerons. The second wing from the top had a gap the width of the fuselage, and the inner ends of the single main spar were connected by a steel tube. The top wing also had a center gap and in addition, had the unique feature of functioning as ailerons. This feature, also used on the Euler V-type triplane, was deleted in favor of conventional ailerons.

Fokker V.8 Septuplane

The most unusual design to emerge from the innovative Fokker works was the five-wing Fokker Model V.8 of late 1917. Using some of the V.6 components this quintuplane was completed on Fokker's order, despite Rheinhold Platz' objections. The addition of the biplane wings at the mid-fuselage position was revolutionary, but quite unsuccessful. Tony Fokker, who did his own test flying, flew it once, had some modifications made, and flew it again. It was never flown again after that and finally was abandoned.

The fuselage had been lengthened, and the 110hp rotary was replaced by a 160hp water-cooled inline

An excellent front view showing the clean lines of the Euler. The German cross on the upper wing shows through the fabric covering. Note the short chords of the four wings, the neat cowling, rotary engine, and sturdy propeller. Peter M. Grosz Collection

Mercedes engine. The standard triplane wings were mounted as far forward on the fuselage as possible, with the engine between the two panels of the center wing. Two modified Dr. I wings with ailerons on the top one were installed as a biplane set between the forward wings and a standard Dr. I tail, with the cockpit just forward of them. A pair of wing-tip skids were located on the bottom wing of the biplane pair.

It is amazing that such a monstrosity ever got off the ground.

Friedrichschafen Quadruplane

Since the Germans had no separate designation for *Vierdeckers* as they did for *Dreideckers*, Friedrich-shafen's second experimental fighter—a one-of-a-kind quadruplane of late 1917—was assigned the official designation of DD. II.

Powered by a 160hp Mercedes D. III engine, it featured four wings of unequal chord with a very unorthodox strut system. The next-to-bottom wing ended at the inside of the inverted V-strut between the bottom and third wing. The neatly streamlined three-ply fuselage was a major departure from the firm's standard practice, and bore a strong resemblance to the Albatros designs. The attachment of the undercarriage to the bottom wing and fuselage was very strange. Unfortunately, the quadruplane never had a chance to prove its worth because it crashed on its first flight. It was later rebuilt as a triplane but was still unsuccessful.

Naglo Quadruplane

The single prototype Naglo quadruplane was built by the German Naglo Bootswerft (Boat works) of Spandau early in 1918, and was accepted by the German Air Force. It was designated the D. II and assigned the serial number 1161/18. While some historians believe that the fourth (bottom) wing was added as an afterthought, it is much more likely it was designed as a quadruplane from the start, since the arrangement of the upper three wings would have been very inefficient for a true triplane design.

Specifications:

Powerplant, 160–180hp Mercedes; span 29ft 6³/₅in (9.0m); wing area 242sq-ft (22.5sq-m); empty weight 1,593lb (720.8kg); gross weight 2,011lb (910.0kg).

Oertz Tandem Quadruplane

The Oertz Schooner followed the Langley concept in having separate tail surfaces behind the short hull that consisted of fixed stabilizer and vertical fins with elevators and rudders. Ailerons were located in the upper forward wing. The W.6 was powered by two 240hp Maybach engines in the hull; each drove a pusher propeller.

The Schooner was completed in June 1914 and was flown to Warnemunde carrying its crew of three, where it was found to be sluggish in the roll. It was modified by installing a second set of ailerons in the rear set of

The big question is, how does one classify the Fokker V.8? Is it a quintuplane or a tandem tri-biplane? Without doubt, it has *to be the most unusual plane designed by the Fokker people, and it certainly is the ugliest!* Bowers Collection

Profile of the Friedrichshafen DD.II quadruplane almost fails to show that there is a fourth wing. The missing wing ended at the triangular strut and on closer inspection can be seen in line with the rear landing gear strut. Heinz J. Nowarra Collection

Even the rear view of the DD.II almost hides the second-from-bottom wing, since it nearly blends with the horizon. It is partially hidden by the elevator. The landing gear was mounted to the enlarged section of the bottom wing, which was unusual. Heinz J. Nowarra Collection

The Naglo D.II quadruplane is almost a three-and-a-half-wing airplane. The bottom wing is attached by a ventral pylon in the center and a pair of N-struts. Joseph Nieto Collection

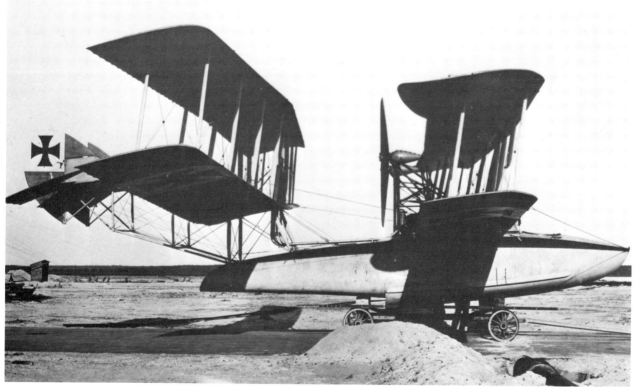

German Oertz W.6 Schooner of 1916, the only successful tandem-wing seaplane of World War I. Visible are the beaching cart and twin pusher propellers. The plane was designed by Max Oertz, a boat designer who had built yachts for Czar Nicholas, Kaiser Wilhelm, and other important historical figures. William Green Collection

wings. Though some reports claim the test pilots thought it was impractical and therefore scrapped, the plane actually was accepted by the German Navy and pressed into service as an unarmed observation plane.

Specifications:
Span 65ft 7½in (20.0m); gross weight 11,066lb (5,007.2kg); top speed 73mph (117.5km/h).

Supermarine Bomber Quadruplane

The Supermarine Night Hawk quadruplane at times was also called the Pemberton-Billings Night Hawk, after Lt. Noel Pemberton-Billings of the RNAS who designed it. Basically designed for night patrol service to hunt for the zeppelins that were raiding London and other vital target areas, it also could serve as a long-range bomber.

The Night Hawk was equipped with an aerial searchlight powered by its own generator to locate the zeppelins and illuminate them for its gunners. The searchlight was gimbal-mounted so that it could be rotated in any direction. Two Lewis machine guns were mounted fore and aft; the rear gunner sat in a cockpit that was level with the top wing and above the main cockpit deck, while the pilot and bombardier were completely enclosed in the cabin which was mounted on the top of the fuselage. The nose gunner's position was in the nose of the fuselage with his gun mounted on a Scarff ring. Both gunners had a wide field of fire. Six double trays of ammo for the Lewis guns plus ten rounds of shells for the single two-pound Davis gun

were standard equipment. The Davis gun was mounted on a double parallel sliding bed, which allowed it to be fired over almost any arc of fire. Each gun was operated by an individual gunner.

The aircraft was equipped with a wireless set. It also had a single bunk so that a crew member could rest or sleep if so disposed. Power was supplied by a pair of ABC air-cooled engines, which left it underpowered. Nine separate fuel tanks were carried, and each one could be used or cut off if damaged by enemy fire, as they were fitted with a new patented fuel tank switching system. All engine controls, pipes, wiring, and so on were on the outside of the fuselage in specially constructed armor-plated casings. All of the wooden parts of the fuselage framework were taped heavily to prevent splintering in case of a crash. The biplane tail had a pair of twin rudders attached. The fuselage was mounted on the second wing from the bottom, as were the engines. These were 100hp Anzani air-cooled radial engines mounted in streamline form nacelles with four-bladed propellers. The landing gear consisted of a pair of double wheels in a standard arrangement, with each set mounted directly under the engines.

The design seemed to be promising despite being underpowered, but after several test flights with test pilot Prodger at the controls it was damaged slightly. But even after modifications to the propellers and changing engines, it was decided to drop the project. However, the quadruplane did fulfill the requirements for operational speed and landing speed specified in the contract.

The large size of the Night Hawk and the difference in wingspan can be seen here. One source stated that the outer wing panels had marked dihedral, though it does not show up *well in this photo. The aircraft had an unusual landing gear arrangement.* Imperial War Museum, London

Saveliev and Zalewski Quadruplane

Wladyslaw Zalewski, a young Pole who had studied at the Wawelberg Technical College in Warsaw, along with his brother Boleslaw, had designed an airplane in 1909 but lack of funds prevented them from obtaining an engine. Zalewski enlisted in the Russian Army and was sent to the Imperial Russian Air Service 2nd Aircraft Park in Warsaw. There he met Vladimir F. Saveliev, the chief mechanic who previously had worked on the giant planes being built at the Russo-Baltic Wagon Works. It was there that the huge Ruski Vitaz and the Ilia Mourometz were built.

The pair got together and decided that future large aircraft should have five or six wings to handle the weight these planes would carry. Zalewski was asked to prepare a study for such a heavy multiwinged bomber, but suggested that the best approach would be to build a smaller single-engine multiplane. It was agreed that would be the best approach, and in November of 1915 the design for the S.Z. quadruplane No. 1 was submitted to the commander in chief. They received a quick approval, and construction was commenced immediately at Smolensk, Russia, the new home of the 2nd Aircraft Park.

Zalewski developed a two-seat quadruplane with wings of diminishing span. The wings were of wood, covered with fabric, and were heavily cambered with a 4deg incidence. The bottom wing had turned-up tips, and the ailerons were fitted on the top two wings only. The fuselage was a wire-braced wooden structure, box-girder type covered with three-ply. The tail was welded-steel tubes and fabric covered. Parts from various types on hand were used including Farmans, Moranes, and even a shot-down German Albatros. To enable it to be flown as a two-seater or a single-seat airplane, the observer's cockpit was placed at the center of gravity in front of the raised pilot's cockpit. A Gnome 80hp seven-cylinder rotary engine was installed, driving a two-bladed propeller of Zalewski's own design.

Taxi trials began on April 23, 1916, with Colonel Jungmeister as test pilot. Things went so well he decided to take off, and made a successful first flight. In later tests it proved to be highly maneuverable and could turn inside a Nieuport Bebe. Top speed was 72mph (115.9km/h). Colonel Jungmeister wanted the quadruplane released for duty, but Zalewski wanted to improve the performance and made a number of modifications before it was once again ready for testing in the fall of 1916. Modified wings with less camber were constructed, the incidence angle was reduced to three degrees, and a larger span and gross area had been fitted. A 100hp Gnome engine now furnished the power. It was even more maneuverable now, and speed had been increased to 82mph (132.0km/h). Despite plans to put it in production, only the one model was built.

In 1918, Zalewski returned to Poland and designed other aircraft between the wars. He also was responsible for several new aero engines.

The S.Z. quadruplane number 2 two-seater was built at the 2nd Aircraft Park in Smolensk, Russia. It was designed merely to gain experience to build a large, multiwing heavy bomber. Heinz J. Nowarra Collection

Prototype specifications:

Span, top 27ft 11in (8.5m), bottom 18ft 1in (5.5m) with 18deg stagger; length 19ft 8in (6.0m); wing area 258.3sq-ft (24.0sq-m); empty weight 794lb (359.3kg); gross weight 1,455lb (658.4kg).

Modified model specifications:

Span 30.5ft (9.3m); wing area 279.9sq-ft (26.0sq-m); gross weight 1,543lb (657.5kg).

Wight Quadruplane

Howard T. Wright joined the firm of J. Samuel White and Company of East Cowes, Isle of Wight, in 1916. He designed several biplane seaplanes for them before the war, so was an experienced designer when he undertook the job of designing a quadruplane fighter as a private venture. One of his seaplanes, the 840, had also been designed for use as a land plane. All of these planes—designed by Howard Wright and built by the White Company—were given the name Wight, after the island where they were built. This quadruplane had three narrow upper chords of equal span, while the bottom wing was 3ft (0.9m) shorter. All wings had rounded tips, and all but the bottom wing were fitted with ailerons. The bottom wing was mounted so close to the ground that it probably acted as a grass cutter while taxiing. All four wings had the typical Wight double-camber airfoil section. Closely spaced double interplane and center section struts were mounted with the struts enclosed by cloth, giving the impression of solid struts. Single flying and landing wires were fitted on each side and connected to the wing spars by metal Y-shaped forms. Notches had to be cut in the bottom wing to accommodate the wheels which were mounted on single struts. A tail skid was mounted on an inverted tripod to hold the tail high enough to keep the bottom wing and tip of the propeller from striking the ground while taxiing. A small tail plane was attached to the top rear of the fuselage. The fuselage was a conventional type similar to the Sopwith triplane. A fully cowled 110hp Clerget nine-cylinder rotary engine drove a two-bladed propeller.

Test trials started in mid-August 1916 with Ralph Lashmar, who was the White Company's test pilot. The plane finally was wrecked in September when Lashmar had to make a forced landing just short of the field at Somerton, and it turned over.

They were able to salvage the engine and some parts. Howard Wright then completely redesigned it in an effort to strengthen and improve its performance. The new design resulted in a wider fuselage with a

This quadruplane is a bit of a mystery ship so far as its designation and time period are concerned, and it seems likely to have been a postwar modification of the S.Z.2. The fuselage is nearly identical to that of the S.Z.2 which *Zalewski, one of the plane's designers, had redesignated the W.Z.III. After the war, he returned to Poland and continued to design and develop other aircraft. J. Alexander Collection*

deeper top deck and an enlarged engine cowl. It incorporated an enlarged fin that extended well forward of the tail plane's leading edge, and a semicircular rudder. The horizontal tail was mounted atop the upper longerons, while the elevator had a cutout to provide room for rudder swing. The wingspan of the three upper wings remained the same, but the bottom wing was increased by 9in (22.9cm). The chord of the top wing was increased 3in (7.6cm), while the other wings retained the same span. The struts were placed a bit farther apart and the cloth fairings were eliminated. Landing and flying wires were doubled and arranged in a more standard form. The lower wing was now completely above the wheels, which now were supported by longer V-struts, and the tail skid was shortened.

The new quadruplane was finished and ready for testing on October 28 but was postponed until November 3 by the Admiralty Air Department. In the meantime, Lashmar was killed in a crash and had to be replaced by an RNAS pilot named Evans, who must have been one of the first "hot pilots" because in an early flight he put on his own air show, diving, looping,

rolling, and zooming all over the sky. Howard Wright watched the performance with misgivings. After the test trials at Somerton, the plane was sent to Martlesham for official testing. By this time J. Samuel White had hired Marcus Manton as his new chief test pilot. Manton had been a test pilot at the Grahame-White Flying School.

While testing the Wight, Manton felt the entire wing cellule shift and made a fast emergency landing. He didn't quite reach the field, so had to crash-land. He escaped serious injury, but the plane was damaged extensively. A new set of wings was designed and built, and it was back in the air again in May 1917. The new wings were moved a few inches aft and their span decreased progressively, with the top wing being 3ft (91.5cm) longer than the bottom one. Only the top two wings had ailerons. The top wing had a chord 6in (15.2cm) greater than the other three. The landing gear wheels were moved farther forward. The new model was ready for trials and was sent to Martlesham for official trials, but nothing happened and it was dismantled and returned to Somerton on September 8, 1918. However, a contract was awarded on November

Second version of the Wight quadruplane at Somerton airfield sometime in early 1917. It was sent to Martlesham

Heath for official tests in February of 1917. Greenborough Associates

13, 1917, but was then canceled and finally written off at Martlesham.

Prototype specifications:

Span, upper three wings 18.75ft (5.7m), lower 15.75ft (4.8m); chord 2.75ft (83.8cm) all wings; gap 2ft 10in (86.4cm); dihedral 4deg; length 20.5ft (6.3m); height 10.5ft (3.2m).

Unidentified Quadruplanes

Last modification:

Wingspan, top 22ft (6.7m), next wing 21ft (6.4m), next wing 20ft (6.1m), bottom wing 19ft (5.8m); chord top wing 3ft (91.5cm), other wings 2.5ft (76.2cm); gap 2ft 7in (78.8cm); dihedral 2.5in (6.4cm); length 21ft (6.4m); height 10.5ft (3.2m); wing area 190.5sq-ft (17.7sq-m); empty weight 872lb (394.6kg); gross weight 1,283lb (580.5kg); top speed 103.5mph (165.8km/h); rate of climb 12min 13sec to 10,000ft (3,048.8m). All models used the 110hp Clerget, and all had a two-bladed propeller 9.25ft (2.8m) in diameter.

An odd feature of this already unusual aircraft is that both propellers rotate in the same direction, contrary to most designs that have a central engine driving two outboard propellers. It has been called Langley Experimental, and seems to have crashed on its first test flight in March of 1919 at

Hazelhurst, an airfield on Long Island at Mineola, New York. This field was bought by Curtiss in 1919 and renamed Curtiss Air Field and eventually merged with Roosevelt Field in 1927. The aircraft was completely demolished in the crash. Art Krieger Collection

Unidentified American twin-float, twin-engine seaplane built in 1916. Note the high wing dihedral. The twin-rudder arrangement is very similar to earlier Burgess designs. Bowers Collection

Chapter 6

Triplanes Between the World Wars

The development of new triplanes after the end of World War I continued, but much of the initial postwar activity involved the testing of wartime designs that had been completed after the Armistice, and the conversion of wartime designs to peacetime use. The only triplane transports to see even limited service were postwar variants of the wartime Caproni Ca. 42.

The only purely military triplanes designed after the war to achieve production status were the US Army's Boeing GAX/GA-1 twin engine ground-attack model of 1920–1922, and the Japanese Mitsubishi 1MT1N Type 10 torpedo bomber of 1922. The latter was designed for the Japanese firm by a British citizen, a former designer for the Sopwith company.

The US Army Air Service developed the world's last giant triplane, the NBLR-1. This six-engine monster first flew in 1923 and was scrapped in 1927 to end the era of the big triplane.

Various firms in the United States and abroad included new triplanes in their postwar development programs, both military and civil, but none ever reached production status. The last serious effort at producing a marketable civil triplane was the tiny American Flea of 1934. It was offered either as a factory-built single-seat sport plane or as a kit "do-it-yourself" homebuilt project.

Twilight of the Triplane

The end of World War I opened up new lines of aircraft activity that had not existed before the war. Triplanes participated in some of these, but never attained the recognition that they had enjoyed during the war. Gradually, the monoplane configuration became dominant. It had been pretty well suppressed during the war by the strength and maneuverability requirements of combat aviation, and the prewar reputation that monoplanes had for structural weakness.

The monoplane became ascendant in the little-known field of gliding. This developed in Germany right after the war because postwar treaty limitations eliminated most forms of aircraft in that country.

In the first experimental years a few triplane gliders were tried, but the monoplane won out and dominated the gliding and soaring scene from 1923 onward. In commercial aviation, the monoplane rap-idly replaced the biplane after proving its economical superiority in the great distance and endurance flights of 1927 and on.

Some of the triplane activity in 1919 was merely completion of developments that had started in 1918. However, some triplane bombers developed during the war were converted to transports in the postwar period to meet the need for passenger airplanes. New triplane designs continued to appear for a few years. Some were major military projects, while others were lesser commercial efforts. The US Army had the distinction of having the last large production triplanes in the world, as well as the world's last triplane heavy bomber. To Italy goes the honor of producing the world's largest triplane, while the last multiengine triplane built by an established aircraft manufacturer took place in the United States in 1927, to close the triplane era.

Army Air Service Engineering Division Triplane

An oddity of US military aircraft procurement in the early 1920s is apparent in the design and building of this unwieldy twin-engine ground-attack triplane.

The Engineering Division of the US Army Air Service often designed new models at McCook Field, Dayton, Ohio. Sometimes industry was invited to bid on building prototypes from Army drawings. At other times the Army built prototypes in its own shops. If the new design was considered to be a desirable production item, the industry was invited to bid for the order.

GAX

Such was the case with the triplane designated Engineering Division Ground Attack Experimental, or GAX. Because of the unorthodox configuration of the airplane and its cannon armament, it was facetiously stated that the GAX stood for "Guns, Armor and X the unknown quantity, as in algebra."

The single GAX, Air Service serial number 63272, was designed by Isaac M. Landon, then an Air Service civilian employee. He was later to achieve fame as the designer of the Consolidated PBY Catalina and the B-24 Liberator of World War II fame, and the giant B-36 Peacekeeper of postwar years.

The GAX structure was conventional, with wood-frame plywood-covered fuselage and wood-frame fab-

The one-only GAX, prototype of the GA-1, was built by the US Army at McCook Field in Dayton, Ohio. The designation

GAX and P-129, the sequential number of test airplanes at McCook Field, appears on the rudder. US Army

ric-covered wings and tail. The forward part of the fuselage housing the two pilots and nose gunner was armored. While the triplane wings were not unusual, the interplane struts were. Each set was a rigid wood frame that had an N-form which eliminated the need for the traditional crossed incidence wires.

The two 400hp Liberty V-12 engines were mounted as pushers in nacelles fitted into and under the middle wing. The nacelles were covered by armor plate, and each housed a gunner with a flexible .30cal machine gun that was aimed through a narrow slit in the armor. The gunner in the fuselage had two flexible 37mm cannons, while the rear gunner behind the wing had a pair of flexible machine guns. A battery of four fixed machine guns pointed forward and down. Ten 25lb (11.3kg) bombs also were carried.

Attack procedure called for the GAX to fly level over ground targets such as troops or cavalry, spraying them with the forward machine guns and cannons rather than diving at a point target and aiming fixed guns by pointing the nose of the airplane at the target as was customary practice.

After testing the GAX in 1920, the Army sought industrial bids on a production lot of twenty. While some bidders did not like the design as such, they needed the business in the early postwar years because cheap surplus planes had stifled the market for new civil designs and there was little demand for new military designs. Much of the existing aviation industry was barely surviving on government contracts for the upgrading of wartime De Havilland observation airplanes for the US Army, and the conversion of DH-4s to mail planes for the Post Office Department, which at that time had a monopoly on the carriage of air mail.

Boeing GA-1

Relatively unknown, the tiny Boeing Airplane Company of Seattle, Washington, was the low bidder and received a contract for twenty production models to be designated GA-1, for Ground Attack Model 1. Air Service serial numbers were 64146–64165.

Even before the first GA-1 was completed and flown in May of 1921, the Army had second thoughts as to the usefulness of the design and cut the order to ten planes.

There is a historical anecdote concerning the first flight of the GA-1, which had to be trucked to Fort Lewis, a large Army post about 40mi (64.4km) south of Seattle since the city had no airfield at that time. The Fort Lewis parade ground was put to use as an airstrip for the test. Army pilots were being issued parachutes by then, but they were in short supply and only a single chute was available to the two pilots who were to test the GA-1. Rather than toss a coin to determine who would wear it, they decided to put it on the floor behind them. If it was needed, whoever managed to get to it first would use it.

Because of the weight and distribution of its armor, the GA-1 was a difficult plane to fly. The pilots could barely see out of the cockpit and the gunners found it extremely difficult to aim their guns through the narrow slits in the armor.

When completed, all ten GA-1s were shipped to the 90th Attack Squadron at Kelly Field, Texas. There were no fly-away deliveries of military aircraft in those days. Deemed useless, the GA-1s had a disciplinary value: Young, hot pilots were cooled off quickly when the squadron commander threatened to assign them to the triplanes.

Boeing-built GA-1 displays the dice insignia of the 90th Attack Squadron while based at Kelly Field, Texas. Bowers Collection

Early in-flight photo of the NBLR-1, commonly called the Barling Bomber, in its original overall olive-drab color scheme. There was a wide separation of the pilot's and copilot's cockpits in the nose, and a slight downward gulling of the narrow center wing. US Army

Unsatisfactory aircraft that they were, the GA-1s have the historical distinction of being the world's last multiengine production triplanes.

Specifications:

Span 65.5ft (20.0m); length 33ft 7in (10.2m); wing area 1,016sq-ft (94.3sq-m); empty weight 7,834lb (3,544.8kg); gross weight 10,126lb (4,581.9kg); top speed 95mph (153.0km/h).

Witteman-Lewis/Barling NBR-1

The Army Air Service Engineering Division was not disillusioned about large triplanes by its GAX/GA-1 experience. In 1920 it hired a British citizen, Walter H. Barling, designer of the ill-fated Tarrant Tabor, to design an even larger triplane, a six-engine bomber. Because of Barling's association with it, the NBR-1 (for Night Bomber Long Range) is often referred to as the Barling Bomber rather than by its official military designation.

The Engineering Division did not elect to build a prototype at this time. A contract for two NBR-1s was awarded to the small Witteman-Lewis Aircraft Corporation of Teterboro, New Jersey. That firm's only recent experience with airplane construction had been the remodeling of war-surplus De Havilland DH-4 observation planes for the Post Office Department.

The NBR-1 was so large that it was built in sections by Witteman-Lewis at Hasbrouck Heights, New Jersey. It was shipped to Wilbur Wright Field, Ohio, and assembled there. Its first flight took place in the early evening of August 23, 1923. The pilots were Lt. Harold R. Harris and Lt. Muir S. Fairchild, assisted by Douglas Culver. Walter Barling rode in the rear upper gunner's cockpit, apparently to prove his confidence in his design. The flight was preceded by a week of taxiing and other ground tests. From his position 15ft (4.6m) above the ground, Barling could see the engines, wings, top of the fuselage, and the tail. He was pleased at the ease with which the plane turned off the taxiway onto the runway as it turned on an axis inside of a wing tip and almost on one undercarriage. He estimated that the takeoff run was about 120yd (109.8m) before the plane climbed out reaching 2,000ft (609.8m), where Harris made a shallow banking turn. Barling then moved forward to watch Culver checking the gauges and electric pumps, while keeping an eye on the engine temperatures, which were rather high because of the small radiators. The electric tachometers were functioning properly. Coming in for a landing later, the plane glided down at about 93mph (149.7km/h), turned into final approach with a normal bank, and settled down so smoothly that Barling could not tell when it actually touched down. The takeoff had taken all of thirteen seconds from a standing start, or eight seconds once full power was applied.

Gen. William L. "Billy" Mitchell, who had pushed strongly for the NBLR-1, in time would hear it called "Mitchell's Folly" because of its extremely short range with a full bomb load. Mitchell saw it as an extremely successful plane from an experimental point of view, but considering its cost of about $350,000 and its disappointing top speed, useful load, and range, no one else supported the project. The range loaded was only 170mi (273.7km), but empty it could manage 335mi (539.35km). Neither figure made much sense for a "strategic bomber," however, and Maj. Henry "Hap"

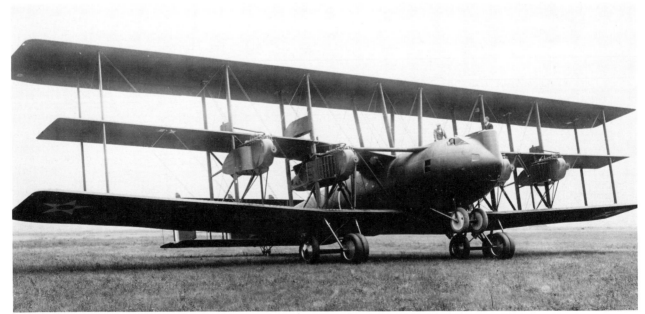

Ground view of the NBLR-1 shows the unique eight-wheel main landing gear. The nose wheels were to protect the nose *in case of a nose-over landing, added strictly as a precaution to avoid a recurrence of the Tarrant Tabor tragedy. US Army*

Arnold, commander of Wright Field in 1927, ordered the prototype burned.

The plane was so underpowered that it could not fly over the Appalachians en route from Dayton to Washington, D.C. It did make a flight from Dayton to St. Louis, Missouri, for the October 1923 National Air Races. One of the refueling stops was at Checkerboard Field in Maywood, Illinois, a Chicago suburb.

One distinction earned by the NBLR-1 was that up to that time it was the largest single object ever carried by an American railroad company. It was so large that it had to be stored at Wright Field over the winter and assembled in the spring. The NBLR-1s flight program ended in 1925. It was never able to climb above 7,000ft (2,134.2m).

The huge cross-laminated spruce fuselage was designed to handle a 2,500lb (1,136.4kg) bomb load and provided positions for a crew of six. The plane had four rudders in a biplane tail, six engines, four mounted as tractors with two-bladed propellers. The other two were mounted as pushers with four-bladed propellers. The engines were 400hp Liberty 12As. The landing gear consisted of ten wheels which barely supported the weight. All engines were mounted between the middle and lower wings. The second prototype was canceled, driving Witteman-Lewis into bankruptcy.

Specifications:
Span 120ft (36.6m); length 65ft (19.8m); height 27ft (8.2m); wing area 4,200sq-ft (389.8sq-m); empty weight 27,703lb (12,535.3kg); gross weight 42,203lb (19,096.4kg); fuel load 2,088gal (7,913.5ltr).

Performance:
Top speed 96mph (154.56km/h) at sea level, 93mph (149.7km/h) at 5,000ft (1,524.4m); cruise at 61mph (98.21km/h); service ceiling 7,725ft (2,355.2m), maximum 10,200ft (3,109.8m) (never attained); rate of climb 19.7min to 5,000ft (1,524.4m), 1min to 325ft (99.1m); range 170mi (273.7km) with a 5,000lb bomb load, 335mi (539.4km) maximum.

Avro 547 Triplane
The British Avro was a commercial triplane that was a prime example of early postwar efforts to produce an enclosed cabin passenger plane by using as many war surplus parts as possible. Except for a new and larger fuselage, all components of the 547 were taken from the Model 504, a 1912 design that had been mass-produced during the war in series up to the 504L model of 1918. Powered by a 160hp Beardmore water-cooled engine the 547 construction was speeded up and cost held down by use of the 504K standard wings, interplane struts, undercarriage, and tail unit. The span was held to a minimum, and the dorsal fin came from a 504L, even though the fuselage was a new design. The plane was built in the same manner with spruce strips and used all the 504K metal fittings, and the fuselage was plywood covered. The cabin could accommodate four passengers or hold 113cu-ft (3.7cu-m) of cargo space for mail or light air-freight packages. The pilot sat in an open cockpit.

Only two 547s were built, G-EAQX and G-EAUJ. Later, G-EAQX was sold to the Australian airline QANTAS in November of 1920. G-EAQX became the

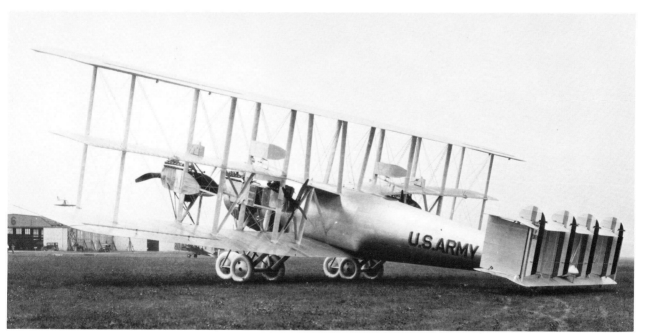

The NBLR-1 after being repainted silver overall, a notable departure from prevailing Army practice. Four-bladed propellers were used on the two pusher engines. US Army

The NBLR-1 being inspected at the Pulitzer races in St. Louis, Missouri, in October 1923. Notice the line of spectators in the background to the left. The Army took the triplane to the air races to obtain publicity: its size was an attention-getter. Fred C. Dickey, Jr., Collection

At the Pulitzer in St. Louis. The landing gear arrangement is clearly visible, as well as the tail wheels. The pair of "emergency" nose wheels became pretty much mandatory after the giant Tarrant Tabor nosed-over on its first attempt at a test flight and killed both pilots. Barling had been a designer on that project and wanted to avoid another such incident. Fred C. Dickey, Jr., Collection

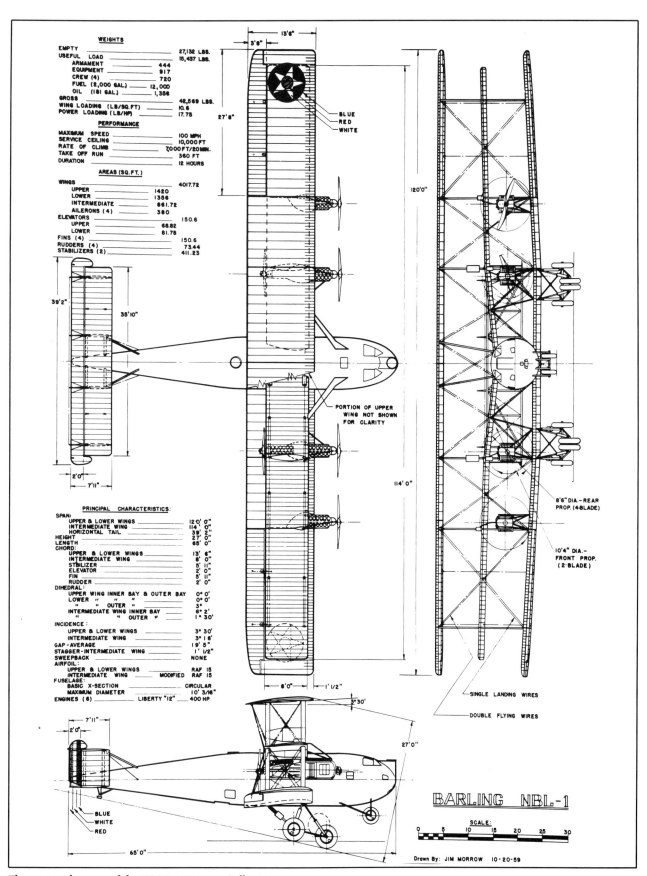

Three-view diagram of the NBLR-1. Bowers Collection

547A after having a 240hp Siddeley engine installed in place of the Beardmore. Entered in the Air Ministry Small Commercial Aeroplane Competition in August of 1920, it qualified for most of the categories but did not win the award because it was unstable and failed to attain the 100mph (161km/h) top speed requirement. The 547 was scrapped in 1921 and the 547A in 1922, but not before both had a number of adventures. The 547A made a hard landing during the competition, and an undercarriage strut was bent so badly that the entire landing gear collapsed shortly afterward when parked in the dispersal area. Later the gear was reinforced to accommodate the heavier weight of the 547A.

After being bought by QANTAS, G-EAQX was registered down under as G-AUCR. It was to have flown the Charlieville-Cloncurry section of the proposed Darwin-Melbourne route. After being shipped to Australia the plane was assembled at Mascot by the Australian Aircraft and Engineering Company, Limited, which replaced the Avro undercarriage legs with a sturdy, rubber-sprung V-strut better suited to the rough landing strips in Queensland. QANTAS entered the 547 in the Australian Aerial Derby, which was held at the Victoria Park Racecourse in Sydney on May 6, 1921. QANTAS manager Hudson Fysh flew the 547 into a second-place finish averaging 69.5mph (111.9km/h). Later on, P. J. McGinniss, the co-founder of QANTAS, was giving demonstration rides at Mascot before leaving for Queensland when the new undercarriage collapsed. This marked the end of 547 and it was cut up for spare parts.

Specifications for 547:

Powerplant, 160hp Beardmore; span 37.25ft (11.4m); length 29ft 10in (9.1m); wing area 498sq-ft (46.2sq-m); empty weight 2,077lb (939.8kg); gross weight 3,000lb (1,357.5kg); top speed 96mph (154.6km/h); cruise 83mph (133.63km/h); rate of climb 15min to 5,000ft (1,524.4m); range 230mi (370.3km).

Specifications for 547A:

Powerplant, 240hp Siddeley Puma; span 37.25ft (11.4m); length 29.25ft (8.9m); wing area 498sq-ft (46.2sq-m); empty weight 2,460lb (1,113.1kg); gross weight 3,800lb (1,719.5kg); top speed 95mph (153.0km/h); cruise 80mph (128.8km/h); rate of climb 19min to 10,000ft (3,048.8m); range 280 miles (450.8km).

Besson Triplanes

The French Besson firm carried its wartime design of triplane flying boats into the postwar years with a two-seat trainer and a single-seat mail plane. Its most ambitious project, however, was a giant four-engine quadruplane flying boat.

H-3 Trainer Triplane

This thoroughly conventional all-wooden pusher flying boat with a 120hp Clerget rotary engine had a side-by-side seating arrangement for two. No production numbers are available, but taking the state of the market at the time, it probably was not developed beyond the prototype model.

Specifications:

Span 28ft 10.5in (8.8m); length 29.5ft (9.0m); wing area 322sq-ft (29.9sq-m); gross weight 1,924lb (870.6kg); top speed 93mph (149.3km/h).

H-6 Mail Triplane

The H-6 was built in 1921 as a low-cost mail plane to operate over the shorter routes where the larger flying boats were not practical. It was an all-wooden aircraft with a 130hp Clerget rotary engine enclosed in a neat nacelle with a very large propeller spinner. The

The first Avro 547 after delivery to the Queensland and Northern Territories Aerial Services, later known as QANTAS, Longreach, Australia. The landing gear was later replaced by a newer style. Civil registration G-AUCR is emblazoned on the fuselage. Note the long exhaust stack. Joseph Nieto Collection

Besson H-3 triplane trainer was a sturdy flying boat of a conventional type and very clean for its time. Notice the heavy tail struts and the wing bracings. Courtesy Alain Pelletier

wing and strut arrangement featured the smallest wing on top to accommodate the wireless wing bracing with single struts sloped inward. It also provided better spacing for the wing-tip floats mounted under the lower wing. Again, this seems to have been a single prototype model.

Specifications:

Span, top wing 20ft (6.1m), center wing 24ft (7.3m), bottom wing 30ft 4in (9.3m); wing area 322sq-ft (29.9sq-m); empty weight 1,320lb (597.3kg); gross weight 1,900lb (859.7kg); top speed 105mph (169.1km/h).

Bristol Transport Triplanes

Pullman

While the Bristol Braemars were intended to be bombers, the third Braemar was fitted with new

The Besson H-6 mail triplane with its unusual wing and strut arrangement and the neat "power egg" nacelle for the engine—a clean, streamlined method of housing the engine. Bowers Collection

The tandem-mounted engines and landing gear wheels of the Bristol Pullman. Originally it was designed as a fifty-passenger transport and eventually was reduced to forty passengers. But the triplane never went into production. Frederick G. Freeman Collection

The Bristol Tramp at Filton, England, in 1922. Actually a testbed aircraft, neither of the two prototypes was ever flown. The four-bladed propellers were to have been driven by transmission shafts from the four Siddeley Puma engines mounted in the fuselage. Bowers Collection

passenger fuselage, renamed the Pullman, and test flown in May of 1920. Although it was not a success, it was given the civil registry G-EASP designation on April 14, 1920, but only carried it until May 13. It was felt that its landing speed was too high to qualify for the Air Ministry Civil Transport Aircraft Competition held in August of that year.

Plans for a fifty-passenger Pullman were laid out by W. T. Reid and scaled down to forty passengers, but since the Air Ministry refused to support the project it never went beyond the prototype stage. One proposal called for using a pair of steam-powered 1,500hp steam turbines. Fraser and Chalmers of Erith embarked on designing a turbine of the Ljungstrom type, while the Bonecourt Waste Heat Company came up with a proposal to design a high-pressure flash boiler. However, their asking price was deemed far too expensive. Thus four Siddeley Tiger engines of 500hp each were used instead, but the project was abandoned anyway.

Tramp

As a result of the Pullman failure, talks continued, and it was decided to build a smaller test-bed triplane. A contract was signed that provided for the design and construction of two prototypes. They were to be powered by four Siddeley Pumas housed in a central engine room, a term usually associated with a nautical rather than an aeronautical project. Siddeley-Deasy Motor Car Company was to supply the gearboxes and transmission shafts. The two Tramps Nos. J6912 and J6913 were completed late in 1921 and neither ever flew because the transmission system, particularly the clutches, gave continual trouble. Work on them was stopped at Filton in February of the following year and they were then shipped to Farnborough for use by the

RAE for experiment and possible further development. Eventually they were written off.

Pullman specifications (fifty-passenger):

Span 81ft 8in (24.9m); length 52ft (15.9m); height 20ft (6.1m); wing area 1,905sq-ft (176.8sq-m); empty weight 11,000lb (4,977.4kg); gross weight 17,750lb (8,031.7kg); top speed 135mph (217.4km/h); ceiling 17,000ft (5,182.9m).

Pullman specifications (forty-passenger):

Span 122ft (37.2m); length 76.5ft (23.3m); height 32.5ft (9.9m).

Tramp specifications:

Span 96ft (29.3m); length 60ft (18.3m); height 20ft (6.1m); wing area 2,284sq-ft (212.0sq-m); empty weight 12,809lb (5,795.9kg); gross weight 18,795lb (8,504.5kg).

Caproni Postwar Triplane Conversions

The Italian Caproni firm made a serious effort at beating swords into plowshares by converting its wartime bombers, both biplane and triplane types, into passenger-carrying transports.

The triplane conversions were relatively simple: Since the narrow nacelles and fuselages were entirely unsuitable for carrying passengers, a large, two-level cabin was designed to fit between the lower and middle wings. The center engine remained in its original location.

Ca.48

The Ca.48 was a twenty-two-passenger conversion of the Ca.42. Seventeen passengers were seated on a bench-type arrangement facing each other across a narrow aisle. The other six passengers rode in the

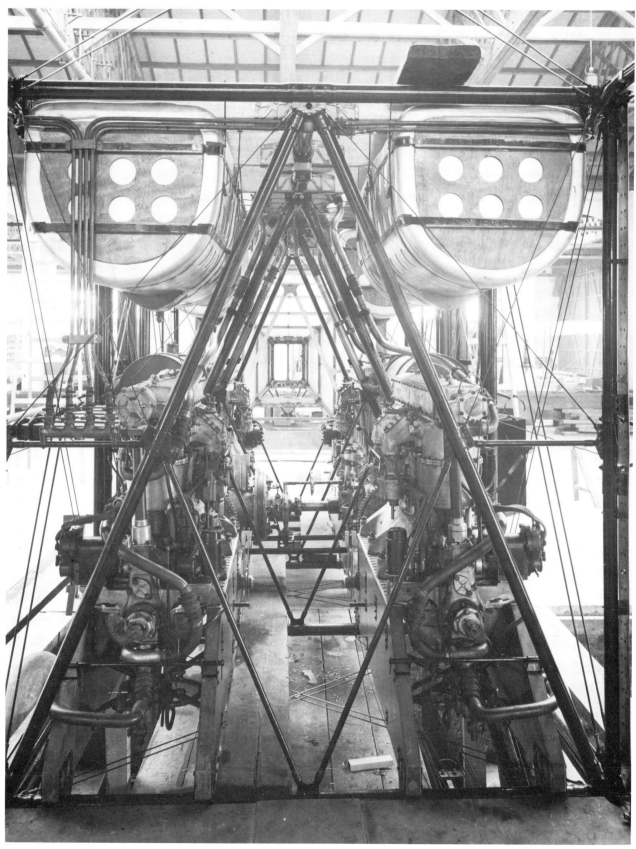

The Bristol Tramp's "engine room" showing the four Siddeley Puma engines mounted in tandem pairs. Fuel tanks were *mounted over the engines. Details of the fuselage construction can be seen.* Bowers Collection

upper-deck cockpit facing forward. Power was provided by either the 300hp Italian Isotta-Fraschini or the 400hp American Liberty engine. The Ca.48 was a trimotor triplane.

Ca.58

The thirty-passenger version of the Ca.48 was designed using five 400hp American Liberty engines. The two outboard engines were installed as pushers in long nacelles that had the standard Ca.42/48 nose radiators ahead of the center wing. For the comfort of the upper-deck passengers, a real cabin was built behind the open pilot's cockpit and projected well above the middle wing.

Catron and Fisk Triplanes

Edward M. Fisk and J. W. Catron formed a partnership in 1917 to produce aircraft in Venice, California. Catron handled the company finances, while Fisk concerned himself with the design and production end of the business. In the 1920s the firm became the world's most prolific producer of triplane designs in the postwar period, turning out four different triplanes between 1921 and 1927. In 1925, the firm was reorganized as the International Aircraft Company and moved to new quarters in Long Beach, California.

Caproni Ca.48, the twenty-two-passenger conversion of the wartime Ca.42 bomber. Female passengers are standing in the open cockpit that forms the upper deck of the between-wings cabin. Bowers Collection

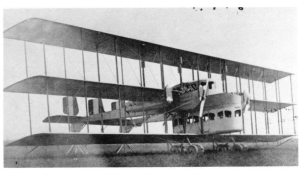

The five-engine Caproni Ca.58 with pusher outboard engines and additional cabin area built above the center wing. The pilots still rode in an open cockpit. Caproni Museum, Italy

The single-seat Catron and Fisk triplane, carrying race number 5, during an air race at Melrose Park, California.

There are ailerons on all three wings. It does have a World War I German look about it. John Underwood Collection

Single-Seat Triplane

Their first airplane design was a single-seat triplane, powered by a Hall-Scott L-6 engine, and built as a racer and sport plane in 1921. Little data is available other than that it was an all-wood airplane. For many years, a single photograph of the plane misidentified as a World War I German Rex was sold to collectors. Since Rex never built a triplane, it does not appear to have been a simple case of mistaken identity.

Trimotor Triplane

This one-of-a-kind triplane was unusual, not only because it was a trimotor but also because it was one of the first designs in America to use automobile engines as powerplants. Model T Ford engines were installed,

one in the nose, and one mounted between the lower and center wings on each side. The lower wing was so close to the ground that wing-tip skids were necessary to keep the wing tip from striking the ground on uneven ground. No other data is available.

Twin-Engine Triplane No. 1

Fisk's first twin-engine design was a redesigned version of the trimotor. It was powered by war surplus Curtiss OX-5 engines. The pilot and passengers sat in open cockpits. The landing gear was spread wider and mounted under the engines rather than under the fuselage, as on the trimotor. This was another one-of-a-kind design.

The Catron and Fisk trimotor triplane with Model T Ford engines. The extremely low position of the bottom wing *resulted in the need for wing-tip skids.* John Underwood Collection

The first Catron and Fisk twin-engine triplane powered by two 90hp Curtiss OX-5 engines. The plane had a wider *landing gear and open cockpit for pilot and passengers.* John Underwood Collection

Twin-Engine Triplane No. 2

In 1926 the firm, renamed International Aircraft, introduced a second and highly refined model still powered by OX-5s. The most notable feature was the octagon plywood-covered fuselage that Fisk had tried on earlier designs and which was to become his trademark on production International biplanes. One contemporary critic remarked that the fuselage was shaped like a rounded coffin. Other differences included an enclosed cabin, a new landing gear with four wheels mounted in pairs under each engine, and a biplane tail with two fins and rudders. The outer wing struts were similar to those of the Sopwith triplane, while the other struts were the N-type. The engines were now housed in streamlined pods. Overall, the structure gave an impression of strength.

In 1927 James D. Dole of the Hawaiian Dole Pineapple company offered $35,000 in prizes; $25,000 to the first pilot to fly from the mainland to Honolulu, and $10,000 to the second person to accomplish the feat. This offer resulted in the event being called The Dole Pineapple Race by the press. Naturally it generated great interest coming on the heels of the Lindberg flight to Paris, and drew a good number of entrants. Among them was the team of James L. Giffin, of Long Beach, California, and Theodore S. Lundgren, of Los Angeles. Giffin was a lawyer who had flown in World War I and remained in the Reserve; Lundgren also was a war veteran and an experienced navigator.

Their aircraft choice was the Catron-Fisk International CF-10 *Pride of Los Angeles*. The CF-10 had been touted as a twenty-two-passenger airliner in 1925. It was specially modified for the Dole race. Its wingspan was 45ft (13.7m), and the Curtiss OX-5s were replaced by Wright 230hp J-5 Whirlwinds. Extra fuel tanks were installed to increase the fuel capacity to just over 600gal (2,274ltr). The pilot and navigator sat side-by-side in an open cockpit near the tail. Giffin's sponsors included at least five southern California businessmen, along with the Hollywood cowboy movie star, "Hoot" Gibson, whose name was displayed in a prominent spot on the nose of the plane. Gibson was quite enthusiastic about the race and not adverse to publicity. The plane was painted a brilliant orange. One story claimed the ship would be able to carry 834gal (3,160.9ltr) of fuel, and plans called for it to fly on to Tokyo, Japan, after it reached Honolulu and was expected to take sixty hours for the trip. Cruising speed was 110mph (177.1km/h).

On August 11 the triplane departed Long Beach for Oakland, California, but made a stop at Fresno to pick up Lawrence Weil, an old friend. Finally at one o'clock in the afternoon, the triplane was coming in as it roared low over the hills southeast of the Oakland airfield, with everyone watching. It touched down on the sandy runway, bounced, and swerved. Giffin opened the throttles to go round again. He circled low and slow over the bay in a downwind turn. Then the left engine sputtered and apparently quit. Being too low, too slow, and flat the plane hit the water and disintegrated. The three men got out of the wreckage unhurt and were helped ashore. That ended the flying

The second Fisk-designed twin-engine triplane had a full cabin in an octagonal-sided fuselage. Engines were Curtiss OX-5s. *It had room for twenty-two passengers.* Ted Lundgren

The 1927 Dole racer—a Catron-Fisk International CF-10 nicknamed Pride of Los Angeles—*after special modifications were made for the race. It was powered by two 220hp Wright*

J-5 radial engines. The center wing does not continue from the engines nacelles to the fuselage. Bowers Collection

The unconventional Louis Clement Sportplane of 1919 on display at the International Salon d'Aeronautique in Paris.

Clement named it the Posoum. *Note the strut and rigging arrangements.* Bowers Collection

career of the *Pride of Los Angeles,* nicknamed "the stack of wheats" by critics.

Clement Triplane Sportplane

The Clement Sportplane was one of the first postwar attempts to produce a light, inexpensive, and safe sport plane. French designer Louis Clement in 1919 established Avions Louis Clement at Boulogne, France, to produce his design.

The design was not copied from anyone and was both unique and original. The single-seat triplane had the main wheels mounted on the wing tips of the lower wing, and a nose wheel was built into the nose of the steel-tube fuselage. A 30hp Anzani radial engine was mounted above the fuselage behind the metal-framed wings, and drove a tractor propeller through a long extension shaft that passed over the pilot's head. Lateral control was maintained by warping the upper and center wing, which was split in the center to allow the propeller shaft to reach the engine.

Specifications:

Wing area 139sq-ft (12.9sq-m); empty weight 198lb (89.6kg); gross weight 374lb (169.2kg).

Curtiss Racing Triplanes

18-T

The 18-T was designed by Charles Kirkham, as a close-air-support fighter. The Navy ordered two prototypes on March 30, 1918. One of the new features was the first monocoque fuselage ever used on a Curtiss airplane. The first prototype, serial number A-3325, had a plywood-covered fuselage and its wings had a thin airfoil and narrow chord using a seven-spar structure without conventional truss ribs, which resulted in a very flexible wing. At first the wings were straight, but when tests indicated the center of gravity was too far aft a 5deg sweep-back was added to the wings, solving the balance problem. Control wires and horns were located inside the plane to reduce drag. The plane was dubbed the Wasp.

On August 19, 1918, with Roland Rohls at the controls the Wasp was clocked at 163mph over a closed course, becoming the fastest fighter in the world. The second prototype A-3326 was entered in the Pulitzer Air Race, along with A-3325 on wheels and with single-bay wings. Prior to this, A-3325 with two-bay wings had established an unofficial world altitude record of 34,610ft (10,551.8m). Floats were added to A-3325, and it set a seaplane speed record of 138mph (222.2km/h) in April of 1920.

Curtiss 18-T (A-3326), with racing number 4 and a yellow paint scheme, rides at anchor while being checked over by a ground crew member who is getting it ready for the 1922 Curtiss Marine Trophy Race at Detroit. US Navy

The Pulitzer race was held at Mitchel Field, Long Island, New York, on November 25, 1920. Lt. Comdr. Willis B. Haviland flew A-3325 while US Marine Corps pilot Lt. W. D. Culbertson flew A-3326. Haviland was forced out of the race on his second lap with carburetor and fuel-line problems. Culbertson lasted until his fourth lap, when he was forced down with a broken connecting rod—but not before he turned in the fastest lap of any of the racers. His first lap had been clocked at 157.495mph (253.567km/h).

After the races both planes were placed in storage until the summer of 1922, when they were taken out and fitted with pontoons and new Curtiss CD-12 400hp engines. Then they were entered in the 1922 Curtiss Marine Flying Trophy Race held in Detroit, Michigan, on October 8, 1922. The course was a 20mi (32.2km)-long triangular track of eight laps. Navy pilot Lt. Rutledge Irvine flew A-3325, and damaged a pontoon in a required landing halfway through the race. He decided to stay in the race but the damaged pontoon broke away, causing the airplane to become uncontrollable and to crash on a coal pile. Irvine escaped injury, but the triplane was a total loss. A-3326, flown by Marine Corps pilot Lt. Lawson H. Sanderson, took the lead and held it until the last lap when he had to land in the water—he had run out of fuel in sight of the finish line.

In October of 1923, with pontoons removed, A-3326 was entered in the Liberty Engine Builders'

Trophy Race at the National Air Races, in St. Louis, Missouri. Its CD-12 engine was overboosted for maximum power, and with Ens. D. C. Allen piloting it, bad luck struck again as the crankshaft broke at the end of the first lap. Allen attempted a forced landing in a field, but it flipped over and was destroyed. The two crew members escaped serious injury and were able to walk away. This accident ended the US Navy's interest in triplanes.

Cactus Kitten

The Curtiss corporation designed and built a racer for Texas oil tycoon S. E. J. Cox of Houston, Texas, for the 1921 Pulitzer Trophy Race. Originally a monoplane, a sister ship to Cox's *Texas Wildcat*, the flaming red *Cactus Kitten* was fitted with triplane wings to bring its landing speed down to within the rule that stated no plane could be entered with a landing speed over 75mph. Clarence Coombs had been selected to fly it. The 1921 race was scheduled to be held in Detroit but was shifted to Omaha, Nebraska, and was flown on November 3, 1921.

The course was a triangular one consisting of five laps at 30.7mi (49.4km) each, for a total distance of 153.5mi (247.1km). It started in Omaha, then on to Carson, Nebraska, then to Loveland, Iowa, and finally back to Omaha. Bert Acosta, flying the Navy's Curtiss CR-1 biplane racer, dueled with Coombs the whole race, and while *Cactus Kitten* was faster on the straight portions, the overly cautious Coombs continually lost

A-3326 at St. Louis, being readied for the Liberty Engine Builders' Trophy Race in October of 1923. Forced to make an emergency landing, Ens. D. C. Allen tried to land in a field, but the plane flipped over and was a total loss. Bowers Collection

Lt. Al Williams and the Cactus Kitten, *which was sold to the US Navy for one dollar and used as a trainer for the Navy's 1923 Pulitzer race team. It was never flown as anything but a* triplane. *You can see the side-mounted radiator, and the Martin MB-1 in the background.* Bowers Collection

World War I German pilot Vicefeldwebel Willi Gabriel, who scored eleven victories while a member of Jasta 11, sitting in the Fokker Dr.I replica built for the German movie D III 88. *One wonders if it was red.* Heinz J. Nowarra Collection

ground thanks to Acosta's skill at cutting the pylons tightly. Acosta won by a scant one minute fifty-eight seconds. Acosta's time set a new world record for a closed-course race. Incidentally, the plane's time of 170mph (273.7km/h) made it the world's fastest triplane of all time.

Specifications:
Wingspan 20ft (6.1m); wing area 210sq-ft (19.5sq-m); top speed 170mph (273.7km/h).

Fokker Triplane Replica
Anticipating the boom in Fokker Dr.I replicas by more than thirty years Alfred Friedrich built a pair of Dr.Is for the German film titled *D III 88*. German World War I ace Vicefeldwebel Willi Gabriel, who was credited with eleven victories in the war, flew it in the movie. The last flyable Fokker Dr.I was borrowed from a museum for this 1930 film production. So the film had the last real Dr.I and the first replica in the air at the same time. It was powered by a British Clerget rotary engine and looked like an original because of careful attention to every detail.

Hanover F.10 Limousine Triplane
The five-passenger Limousine produced in 1919 by the German firm of Hannoverische Waggonfabrik Aktien Gesellschaft was unusual on several counts. Like the other well-known German firms that struggled to survive by producing quickie passenger adaptations of their wartime two-seaters, Hanover gave thought to following suit but decided that they would have a better opportunity with an entirely new postwar civil transport model. While three other manufacturers were trying new monoplane designs, Hanover went with a triplane offering.

The F.10 triplane followed contemporary practice by seating four people facing each other in a limousine-like rear cockpit, hence the name, while the fifth passenger rode up front in the open cockpit with the pilot.

The use of the biplane tail was a carryover from Hanover's wartime models. The most unusual thing about this triplane is that unlike all others, the top wing was the smallest while the center and lower wing each increased in size, the exact opposite of standard practice.

The airplane division of the big Hanover firm was a sideline that soon was discontinued early in the postwar years, while the parent company grew and prospered.

Specifications:
Powerplant, 230hp Benz; span (bottom wing) 37ft 10³/₈in (11.5m); length 26ft 6⁵/₈in (8.1m); wing area 484.2sq-ft (44.9sq-m); empty weight 2,375lb (1,074.7kg); gross weight 3,780lb (1,710.4kg); top speed 106mph (170.7km/h) at 6,500ft (1,981.7m).

Kauter Flying Boat Triplane
The Kauter Triplane flying boat is somewhat of an enigma since data on it is impossible to locate. Not even the designer's name, or company of manufacture are recorded. The plane itself offers no clues in the way of serial numbers, registration numbers, and so on. Since

The five-passenger German Hanover F.10 Limousine triplane of 1919. The single flying wire on each side of its biplane horizontal tail extends from the lower wing to the upper, *while the corresponding landing wire extends only from the center to the lower wing. The aileron was fitted to the lower wing only.* Bowers Collection

The Kauter triplane flying boat, floating behind a yacht on a river. Distinguishing features include a diminishing wingspan, wing-tip float attached closely to the bottom wing, and extensive wire rigging on the wings. The outer wing struts are slanted outward. John Underwood Collection

it is tied up to a large yacht whose name on the stern cannot be read, it would seem to have been used as a pleasure craft by its owner.

For the most part the design is a straightforward pusher flying boat of medium size, with a four-bladed propeller. The engine is either a 400hp Curtiss CD-12 or a 435hp Curtiss D-12. The only unusual external feature is the biplane tail assembly with two sets of stabilizers and elevators. The design is a clean one. Ailerons on the top two wings is standard practice on triplanes. The upper wing surfaces, elevators, stabilizers, upper hull, and tip of the tail seem to have been painted a dark color.

Komta Triplane

The Komta was a Russian triplane designed to be used as a bomber or ten-passenger transport plane. The twin-engine triplane was designed in 1920 under the auspices of Komta, and tested in May of 1922. It was powered by a pair of 240hp Fiat engines that propelled it to a maximum speed of only 87mph (140.1km/h). It was produced at Factory No.1.

The Komta was basically a land plane, but provisions were made to fit it with skis in keeping with the harsh Russian winters. The wings were staggered to the rear, with the center and lower wing being of equal span while the top wing was longer. Ailerons were fitted on all three wings and a biplane tail was used. When used as a land plane, the gear had two wheels on each side. Two-bladed propellers were fitted to the engines, which were mounted between the two lower wings.

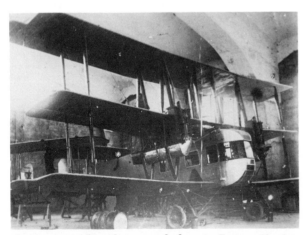

The Komta triplane being worked on in Factory No. 1 in Russia. Apparently this one was a modification, as the overhanging aileron on the lower wing does not appear on the other aircraft. The propellers have not been attached and the aircraft itself is lifted off the floor by a sawhorse under the rear of the fuselage, and small logs under the landing gear. Heinz J. Nowarra Collection

Mitsubishi Type 10 Torpedo Triplane

After World War I the Mitsubishi Company invited British engineer Herbert Smith, at the urging

The finished Komta rests on skis out in the open, being readied for flight trials. The enclosed cabin looks cozy and must have been enjoyed by the pilot and crew members. Heinz J. Nowarra Collection

The Japanese Navy's first triplane, the Type 10, was meant to be a carrier-based airplane. It also was the only triplane ever produced in Japan. A solid aircraft it initiated the Kanko, or high-performance carrier-attack aircraft category in the Japanese Navy. Bowers Collection

of the Japanese Navy, to come to Japan to design aircraft for them. He designed a fighter and a reconnaissance type, which were accepted, and was then requested to design a single-seat torpedo bomber based on his other efforts. His design was a wooden structure with fabric covering, with equal-span two-bay triplane wings. The wings were nonfolding, which was a bit strange for a plane designed to operate off of a carrier since the wingspan was almost 44ft (13.4m). The pilot sat in an open cockpit. The triplane design was chosen for its ability to carry a torpedo as a payload, and for its maneuverability. Since the plane was designed in 1921, which was the tenth year of *Taisho*, all designs that year received the Type 10 designations and were only differentiated by their mission roles so it can be confusing.

The prototype was completed in 1922 and on August 9, test flown by William Jordan at the factory airfield. In November, the first and second prototypes were flown by Japanese Navy pilots at Kasumigaura and were accepted by the Navy. While it outperformed competitors in climb rate and maneuverability it failed to live up to expectations, but the pilots liked its flying characteristics and general maneuverability. Because of its height, it was difficult to handle on the ground. Despite this, twenty Type 10s were built, to become the world's last production triplanes.

One was later converted to a floatplane by Ando Aeroplane Research Studio at Shin-Maiko Beach, Chita Peninsula, in 1926 and used as a transport and trainer. On July 4, 1924, Lieutenant Kikuchi set an altitude record for Japan, reaching 25,000ft (7,622m). The first successful torpedo launch took place on December 5, 1924.

Specifications:
Powerplant, 450hp Napier Lion twelve-cylinder water-cooled engine driving a two-bladed wooden propeller; span 43.5ft (13.3m) equal span; length 32ft 1in (9.8m); height 14ft 7.5in (4.5m); wing area 462sq-ft

(42.9sq-m); empty weight 3,020lb (1,366.5kg); gross weight 5,511lb (2,493.7kg); top speed 130mph (209.3km/h); cruising speed 81mph (130.4km/h); rate of climb 13.5 minutes to 10,000ft (3,048.8m); service ceiling 19,685ft (6,001.5m); maximum 19,800ft (6,036.6m); endurance 2.3 hours; armament one 18in (45.7cm) torpedo.

Parnall Possum Triplane
At the end of World War I the British Air Ministry's Directorate of Technical Development issued a proposal for a special cargo-carrying aircraft to serve a medium-range postal role. George Parnall's chief designer Harold Bolas designed an airplane for this role, but also included a possibility to convert it to military use should the need arise. Bolas decided to use a triplane configuration to enable the drives from the fuselage to be housed in the middle wing. At the time the British leaned toward mounting engines in the fuselage to drive propellers through gearing and a

The first Parnall Possum, serial number J6862. Number 10 was its exhibit number for the RAF Hendon Air Pageant held on June 28, 1923. Notice the radiator on the fuselage. Greenborough Associates

system of extension driveshafts. The design received the name Possum.

The single 450hp Napier Lion was located inside the flat-sided plywood fuselage at the center of gravity. The three-cylinder blocks of the engine were left out in the open, while power to the two outboard 9.5ft (2.9m) diameter wooden propellers was transmitted through a bevel gear drive to shafts in the leading edge of the middle wing. The shafts were completely encased and ran between the leading edge and front spar. The propellers were contrarotating.

The reduction gears and shafting were produced by D. Napier and Sons, who also made the Lion engine. Radiators were placed on each side of the fuselage and hinged to allow the radiating surfaces to be turned by the pilot from his cockpit to enable him to regulate the engine cooling rate. The water header tank and a large gravity-feed fuel tank were incorporated in the center section of the top wing. The Possum had a swiveling tail wheel with an automatic brake. Brake friction progressively increased as the load on the tail wheel increased, but the pilot could release the brake from the cockpit.

The Possum's wings were of equal span and unstaggered. All three wings had symmetrically balanced, long-span, cable-controlled ailerons. The Possum was an all-wooden airplane, and wings and tail surfaces were fabric covered. The wings were strut and wire braced. The undercarriage had an oleo-type mounting with the wheels being widely spaced on a cross axle. Finished in 1923, the Possum made a couple of ground hops before making its first official flight on June 19, 1923. Wing Commander Norman MacMillan was the test pilot and Harold Bolas, showing confidence in his design, went along as a passenger since he wanted to observe the drive system in action.

The Possum was quickly tried as a military aircraft. The front and rear cockpits were given Scarff gun mountings. The plane carried a radio, photo-graphic equipment, and even a rocket-firing device. A parachute housing compartment was located so that the crew could reach it quickly. The Possum also was put through a series of bombing and reconnaissance trials.

It was flown to RAE Farnborough on April 15, 1924, and painted silver overall to appear at RAF Hendon on June 28 at the Air Pageant. After some delay the second Possum was finished and flown at Yale Aerodrome on April 27, 1925. It too was painted all-silver and also appeared at the Hendon Air Pageant. Both Possums were flown at Martlesham for some time before being taken off inventory.

Specifications:

Span 64ft (19.5m); length 39ft (11.9m); height 13.75ft (4.2m); wing area 777sq-ft (72.1sq-m); gross weight 6,300lb (2,850.7kg); top speed 105mph (169.1km/h); cruising speed 80mph (128.8km/h).

Ricci Triplane

The Ricci R.6 triplane was an Italian design built in Naples right after World War I. It was inspired by the Caproni-Breda-Pensuti Messenger, which was an attempt to build the world's smallest airplane.

The Ricci 6 was modified several times during its short career. It was an equal-span triplane with ailerons mounted on the top and bottom wings. The tail skid was exceptionally long. The bottom wing was mounted under the fuselage very close to the ground, which made the long tail skid necessary.

Richter Triplane Glider

The triplane glider built by Friedrich Richter is representative of the many configurations tried when the German glider movement began in 1920 as a result of the restrictions on powered aircraft operations imposed by the Allies.

While the performance of the Richter design was little better than that of the hang gliders built near the turn of the century, it made an 8.5-second flight on September 7, 1920, which ended in a crash-landing. It

The original Ricci R.6 ready for a test flight. The test pilot must have been superstitious because he had a Kewpie doll tied on the right cabane strut. You can see the Italian Air Force cockade on the rudder and the word Napoli *underneath it, with the designation R.6 above it. The name* Ricci *is repeated on the fuselage. The rudder shape is different from other models.* Bowers Collection

This R.6 was on exhibit at an air display in France. The R.6 designation on the rudder is different, having been rounded off, and a pair of diagonal stripes have been added to it. The word Napoli *has been reduced and relocated on the rudder.* Alberto Casirati Collection

was still a significant milestone in glider development, however. In contrast to the hang gliders, the pilot was seated and operated conventional-type airplane controls instead of by shifting his weight.

The main contribution made by Richter was his convincing demonstration that multiple wings were not suitable for gliders. Aerodynamic interference between the surfaces, plus the necessary struts and rigging, proved to be major drag handicaps. All subsequent gliders and sailplanes of any significance have been monoplanes.

Specifications:

Span 13ft 4in (4.1m).

Sarotti SP-5 Triplane

An interesting throwback to World War I was the Sarotti SP-5 triplane of 1925. Built in Germany as an individual project by Max Schuler, it appears to be a rebuilt Fokker Dr.I using the original fuselage and landing gear. The wings were rebuilt, using differently shaped wing tips and additional ribbing. The nose section had an obvious spliced-in section to move the lighter-weight 80hp Swedish Thulin rotary engine forward to maintain balance. The tail surfaces were reshaped and a small vertical fin was added.

Since it was sponsored by the Sarotti Chocolate Company, which used it for advertising, it was given their name. The SP-5 appeared in World War I aviation movies in Germany in the 1930s.

This bottom view of the R.6 shows the wing details, rigging, ailerons, and landing gear. This plane has been restored and is now in the Milan Technical Museum. Alberto Casirati Collection

Another view of the Ricci 6 in the Milan Museum. Note the rudder stripes, the fuselage striping, the wheels with a circle on the hubs, and that the name now appears on the rear of the fuselage. The shape of the rudder has been changed slightly. Alberto Casirati Collection

Although the identity of this triplane is unknown it seems more than likely that it was the final version of the R.9. It is pictured here at a French Aero Meeting in the early 1920s. Apparently a new engine was installed and moved a bit forward, and a cowling was fitted. The cockpit also has been moved forward. Judging from the crowd in this photo, air shows were popular in those days too. Alberto Casirati Collection

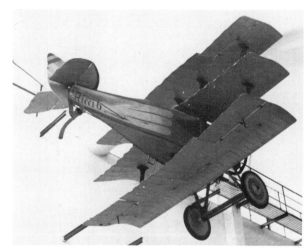

The Ricci R.9 on display at the Paris Aeronautical Salon in the 1920s. The R.9 differed from the R.6 by being a two-seater. The tail and rear fuselage have been redesigned, and the engine neatly cowled. It was obviously being offered as a sport plane. Bowers Collection

Friedrich Richter during his 8.5-second flight at Wasserkuppe, Germany, on September 7, 1920—just seconds before the crash. The glider had twin rudders and skids under the wings. Wolfgang B. Klemperer

Universal Aircraft Company American Flea Triplane

The American Flying Flea triplane was developed by the Universal Aircraft Company of Fort Worth, Texas, in 1934. It was designed and produced by Lillian Holden and test flown by Ragan Ormond. It was then offered as a kit with an easy down-payment plan of $12.50. The company also offered propellers and other supplies at factory prices. A factory-built Flea sold for $695. Ormond claimed that it would outperform a $1,500 ship, that it did not stall, and had everything one could want in a sport plane.

The Continental A-40 was the preferred engine, but other engines were fitted at various times including a 65hp Lycoming and a 65hp Continental A-65 engine. It was a single-seat triplane based on the French-designed Mignet Pou De Ciel (Sky Flea), a 1935 sport plane. The Universal Aircraft Company ceased operations in 1942 after the outbreak of World War II. Later George Frisbie of DePere, Wisconsin, tried to resurrect it after World War II and offer it as a kit.

The Sarotti SP-5 was a rebuilt Fokker Dr.I with modified wings and tail. The nose was lengthened to move the lighter 80hp Thulin rotary engine ahead of the original position of the Oberursel in order to maintain proper balance. Pictured at an exhibition in May 1925, two Junkers can be seen in the background. Bowers Collection

Universal Flea specifications:

Span 20ft (6.1m); length 13ft (4.0m); empty weight 350lb (158.4kg); cruising speed 85mph (136.9km/h); stall speed 30mph (48.3km/h).

Frisbie Flea specifications:

Span 20ft (6.1m); length 15ft (4.6m); top speed 100mph (161km/h) (approximately).

Flying Whatever ? Triplane

It has been said that a photo is worth a thousand words, but this photo raises a thousand *questions*. This triplane looks to have been very well constructed of steel tubing, which probably was to have been fabric covered. The triplane wings are unconventional to say the least, and have a most unusual arrangement. An 80hp LeRhone engine and a Thomas Morse S-4C propeller are clearly World War I surplus, while the landing gear style is one that evolved in the late 1920s.

The purpose of the streamers on the wings is unknown, but may have been used for some sort of wind-tunnel testings to study the airflow. These are things one would expect to find on an ornithopter. Could this have been an attempt at one? Judging from the snow on the ground and the word *Colorado* on the back of the print, this possibly could have been conceived in that state.

Unknown Triplane

This unidentified triplane apparently was built in Chicago in the late 1930s, but nothing is known about the designer. Mounting an aircraft or automobile on a roof of a gas station, hamburger stand, or small business was always an attention grabber and was common in Chicago back then, so there is nothing unusual about this display.

Provision for the lower wing can be seen between the letters H and E in the sign. The propeller seems to just be mounted for effect as no engine seems to be left

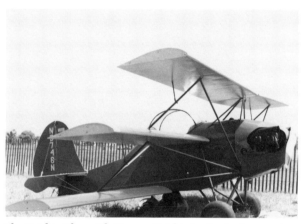

The Frisbie Flea with George Frisbie in the background, at an Experimental Aircraft Association Fly-In at Rockford, Illinois. The Frisbie Flea differed from the Universal Flea by being 2ft (61cm) longer and having squared-off wing tips. Art Krieger Collection

The Frisbie had a regular wind screen, but also had a canopy, apparently to keep out rain. The entire bottom wing served for an aileron control. Art Krieger Collection

The Frisbie's unusual strut configuration resulted in a strong aircraft. While the wings of the Universal Flea were all of equal span, on the Frisbie they were of decreasing span. Art Krieger Collection

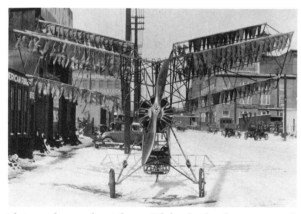

Flying whatever? triplane. While the landing gear style seems to indicate a plane of the 1920s and most of the autos in the background are of that era, the one behind the fuselage is a 1930s' model car. The plane is parked in front of the American Forge Company. Courtesy Joseph P. Juptner

in the fuselage, possibly to reduce weight on the roof of the station. Several small dents and nicks probably were made while positioning it. The fuselage of corrugated metal would have lent strength to the plane. The fin and rudder seem to be copies of the Sopwith triplane. The instrument panel, stripped of anything that may have been installed, was located above the cockpit in a most unusual position.

Another experimental triplane of the 1930s. This one ended up on the roof of a Shell gas station near Narragansett Avenue and Northwest Highway on the north side of Chicago. Nothing is known of its history. Art Krieger Collection

Chapter 7

The Last Multiplanes

The period after World War I produced some of the largest multiplanes as well as some of the oddest. Some designers who thought in terms of the airplane as a means of transporting passengers and cargo over long distances safely, rapidly, and in comfort while turning a good profit. Some thought that only huge airplanes could fulfill these goals. The companies that at least attempted to do so, included Caproni and Besson and an individual named John. These people turned out three gigantic airplanes, none of which lived up to expectations of the designers.

On the other hand others who thought the multiple wings were the answer to overcoming other problems; Gerhard hoped to be the first person to fly using only human power, a dream that was not to be realized until five decades had passed and then not by a multiplane. A few others continued to tinker with these types but none were really successful. The age of multiplanes was coming to an end but it had at least been an interesting one.

Besson H.5 Quadruplane

Marcel Besson continued his postwar flying boat developments with his Model H.5 which, of all his achievements, was the most spectacular. It was completed and tested at St. Raphael, France, in 1922. Designed as a twenty-passenger transport, it was the world's largest quadruplane. It had a number of unconventional features incorporated in the design.

Side view of the Besson H.5 showing the unusual arrangement of the four wings and the separate flotation structure below the fabric-covered fuselage. Posing a small airplane alongside a larger one to emphasize the size of the latter was common practice. The smaller craft is a Nieuport 11 fighter.
Bowers Collection

First, the hull was not a true flying boat type, but had been designed as a boat to give it better handling qualities in the water. It was a laminated wooden structure that, in effect, was a large, single pontoon attached to the fuselage at ten attachment points rather than being supported below it by struts. Besson also had proposed to attach an undercarriage to convert it to a land plane should that be advisable or desirable.

The equal-span wings were mounted, in effect, as two pair of biplane wings. The top and third-from-top wings were in line with each other as were the other pair, the bottom and second-from-top wings. However, the pairs were staggered, with the bottom and second-from-top wing being placed almost a chord aft of the other two. This unusual treatment had several advantages. First, it reduced the interactions of airflow to a minimum. Second, this staggering had the advantage of locating the rear propellers of the pusher-puller engine pairs, housed in long nacelles on the next-to-bottom wing ahead of the trailing edge of the bottom wing, to protect them from spray thrown up during takeoffs and landings. Third, this arrangement permitted a reduction in the amount of wire rigging. The structure was perfectly rigid, even with its 2,424.6sq-ft (225sq-m) wing area. Power was furnished by four Salmson 9Z engines, though provision had been made to eventually substitute the 370hp Lorraine engines. But this was never carried out. The H.5 carried a crew of five, plus twenty passengers.

Another aerodynamic feature years ahead of its time was the use of the small upper surface of the biplane tail assembly as a longitudinal trimming device, not as a fixed stabilizer or movable elevator.

Specifications:

Span 95.1ft (29m); length 72.1ft (22m); height 21.3ft (6.5m); wing area 2,424.6sq-ft (225sq-m); empty weight 12,155lb (5,500kg); gross weight 22,100lb (10,000kg); maximum speed 106mph (170km/h); cruising speed 90mph (145km/h); range 559mi (900km).

Caproni Ca.60 Multiplane

Ing. Gianni Caproni, a pioneer of Italian aviation, started designing large-size heavy bombers in 1913 for the newly formed Aviazione del Regio Esercito (Royal Army Air Service). His biplane and triplane bombers saw extensive action in World War I and performed well. When the war ended Caproni decided to build the world's largest airplane, one capable of carrying 100 passengers from Europe to the United States. He began working the design in 1919. He knew safety and reliability was of paramount importance and since it would be flying over vast areas of ocean, the airplane would have to be a seaplane.

The new plane would be the Caproni Ca.60 Transaereo but also came to be called unofficially Noviplano and Capronissimo, in awe of its huge size. Basically, Caproni had to design a new hull large enough to comfortably accommodate 100 passengers. The hull was approximately 71.5ft (21.8m) long and covered with plywood; the bottom portion was given a double covering of plywood for extra strength. Three sets of triplane cellules of equal dimensions were to be connected to the hull. These triplane wings were left over from wartime bomber production. The combined area of the nine wings was 9,000sq-ft (835.2sq-m). Only one airplane ever exceeded that total, the Hughes

Called the Flying House Boat, the Caproni Ca.60 floats on Lake Maggiore in northern Italy. The open door of the passenger entrance is at the stern. The Macchi M.7 flying *boat in front of the Capronissimo gives some idea of the huge size of the Ca.60. Bowers Collection*

Spruce Goose H-4 flying boat. By coincidence, both of these behemoths achieved flight and about the same altitude in their first and only flights.

The center wings of each triplane set were connected by two wooden auxiliary fuselages. Each one of the parallel auxiliary fuselages contained two 400hp Liberty engines at each end. A power nacelle containing one pusher and one tractor engine was placed between the fuselages at the front and rear wing sets. Thus the total of eight engines consisted of four tractor and four pusher engines. The auxiliary fuselages served as passageways to enable mechanics to make minor repairs or adjust the engines in flight. Ailerons were placed on all nine wings, but those on the rear set served as elevators. Vertical fins and rudders were mounted between all the rear wings. Two large floats were mounted under the lower wing of the middle set of wings.

A unique arrangement provided for a specialist in the engine nacelle who would take care of the engines. He could communicate with the cockpit by a series of colored electrical lights. Fuel tanks were located in the middle of the hull, and the fuel was pumped up to smaller gravity tanks located over the engine. The engines in the nacelles drove four-bladed propellers, while the engines in the auxiliary fuselages drove two-bladed types. The cockpit was open and was located at the nose with side-by-side seating for the pilots. A commander's room was placed to the rear of the cockpit to provide space for the navigation equipment and maps. The hull housed the passenger seats, toilets, and a bar. The 144 struts gave rigidity to the structure.

Caproni had to build a special hangar in which to construct the giant plane, and construction was started in 1920 at Sesto Calende, a small town on Lake Maggiore in northern Italy. The Transaereo was completed in February of 1921, and the first flight was scheduled for the beginning of March. The test pilot,

Closeup of the nose of the Transaereo Ca.60 shows the arrangement of the Liberty engines in the forward nacelle, and the tractor Libertys in the front ends of the full-length parallel auxiliary upper fuselages. This arrangement was repeated in reverse order between the rear wings. Alberto Casirati Collection

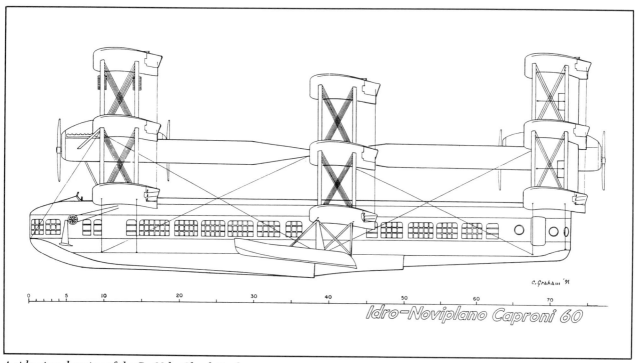

A side-view drawing of the Ca.60 by Chuck Graham

Sempirini, decided to fly it even though Caproni was away on business. So he ordered 3,315lb (1,500kg) of sand poured into the hull. Sempirini, along with three mechanics, boarded the plane for the test flight. After a long run it finally became airborne and climbed to an altitude of about 80ft (24.4m), flew straight and level a short while, then banked and crashed. Sempirini seemed to have lost control in the bank, due to shifting of the sand ballast.

Though no one was injured, the plane was badly damaged. It was never repaired because it was de-stroyed in a hangar fire. Thus ended the Ca.60, which was the first eight-engine airplane in the world.

The probable cause of the crash was that the plane's center of gravity was off. It simply was not strong enough to withstand the impact against the lake surface.

Specifications:

Powerplants, eight 400hp Liberty engines; span 98ft 5in (30.0m); length 76ft 11¼in (23.5m); height 30ft (9.2m); wing area 7,696sq-ft (714.2sq-m); gross weight

Looking much like a child's attempt to build a tissue-covered rubber-band powered flying model airplane, the Gerhard Cycle plane sits on a concrete circle. A forerunner to the Gossamer Albatros, *it looks ready to collapse under its own weight.* US Army

55,000lb (24,886.8kg); estimated top speed 81mph (130.4km/h); cruising speed 68mph (109.5km/h); range 410mi (660.1km).

Gerhard Cycle Multiplane

Inventor Gerhard designed a seven-wing human-powered airplane in the early 1920s at McCook Field, Dayton, Ohio. Gerhard felt that he had a new approach that would solve the problems of earlier designs, which were beset with poor aerodynamics. He was aware that high-aspect-ratio wings had less induced drag. He also knew that for a practical wingspan, high aspect ratio also reduced the area. His idea was to simply add more wings and thought that seven wings would solve the problem. For some reason he chose to ignore the fact that struts and rigging added drag, and that past experience had shown that the interference drag between adjacent wings pretty much limited such designs to three wings.

In lieu of a powerplant, the Cycle's propeller was driven by the pilot pedaling a bicycle. When the plane was tested the entire wing structure simply collapsed about the pilot, who managed to escape injury. The wings failed as soon as they tried to lift off. The entire test was filmed and has been featured many times in aviation history films or in comedy short subjects, as well as news reels of the time.

The lack of flying and landing wires to take the wing loads doomed the project from the start. He did attempt to keep the plane as light as possible, but this only further limited the strength of the entire structure. Elevators were mounted on the bottom wing only. A human-powered aircraft capable of flight was still years in the future.

Johns Multiplane

Would-be designer Herbert F. Johns had the foresight to recognize that World War I eventually would create a requirement for a large airplane capable of carrying heavy loads, and so decided to design one of his own. His research indicated that the strength of available materials and technical state of the art, versus the current weight restrictions, would limit wingspan to roughly 140ft (42.7m) maximum. To get around this limitation, he decided to increase the wing area and thus increase lift by adding more wings. According to his calculations, seven wings should solve the problem. This concept, Johns reasoned, offered the promise of an airplane capable of handling a tremendous payload without creating an extremely large one.

When he approached the Army Air Service in 1916 with his proposal to build such a plane, those in charge were skeptical since no septuplaned had ever been built up to that time. The Army had its doubts but since he stated that it would be built with private funds, they agreed to test and evaluate it upon completion and even to allot the engines to the project when it was ready for them. They had nothing to lose, and they had doubts that he would ever complete it.

Johns then proceeded to form the American Multiplane Company in Bath, New York, and soon construction work was under way. The plane was to have a gross weight of 10,000lb (4,524.9kg), a crew of five, and be powered by three engines, two being mounted as pushers and the third in the nose as a tractor. These engines were to be furnished by the government. The main wing assembly was to be a tri-plane, with a set of biplane wings mounted ahead and behind the main wings. More than sixty struts would

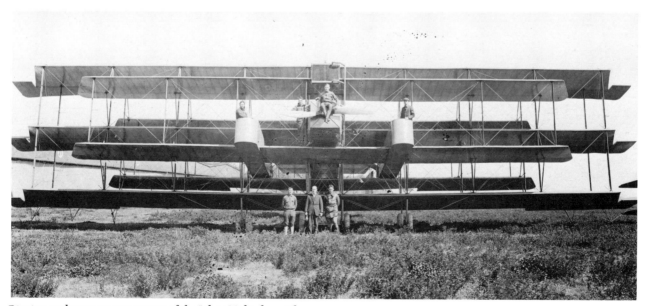

Rigging and strut arrangements of the Johns Multiplane. The gunners' stations in the nacelles have men standing in them.
Bowers Collection

be used to hold the wings together in an interlocking system. The tail was a biplane unit with three rudders, and the main gear consisted of six wheels with a pair mounted under each engine nacelle and the remaining two mounted under the fuselage. In addition, a pair of tail wheels were positioned under the tail section. The wire rigging created a complex maze resembling a bird cage. The engine nacelles also housed a gunner.

In March of 1918 the Air Service sent inspectors to the plant to check on progress at the request of Johns. They found the Multiplane partially completed, and concluded the construction work was sound and would be acceptable. In April, a Mr. Potter relayed Johns' request for three 400hp Liberty engines to Col. Jess G. Vincent at McCook Field. Colonel Vincent ordered the engines shipped from McCook, but advised Johns that there were no facilities at McCook to assemble the plane and suggested that he try Buffalo, New York, as it might be a suitable site closer to his plant. Johns

learned that it could not handle the plane either. Finally in August of 1918, Wilbur Wright Field in Ohio was selected for the assembly and test site, and the plane was crated and shipped there by rail with the understanding that a facility would be built for the purpose. The war ended before the construction got under way and the Army's interest cooled on the project. The Multiplane was shipped on to Langley Field, Virginia, in 1919 because a large hangar was available there. It arrived in January and was stored until spring, and finally assembled in June.

Lt. Raymond W. Hamilton, a pilot with extensive experience flying multiengine aircraft, was assigned as the test pilot. He made a number of taxi runs to get the feel of the giant plane. On the morning it was scheduled to make its first flight, Gen. Billy Mitchell arrived in his personal De Havilland leading a flight of four, with each plane carrying two mechanics in the rear cockpits. Colonel Hensley met the general in his staff car, accompanied by two trucks to haul the mechanics and

The Johns Multiplane at Langley Field, Virginia, on April 25, 1919, ready for the test flight. Pictured are the interlocking *struts, the long dorsal fin, and the landing gear arrangement.* USAF

Side view of the Johns shows the relationship between the sets of wings, the biplane tail, rear wheels, and long dorsal fin.

Ailerons were mounted on all three triplane wings. Fred C. Dickey, Jr., Collection

their equipment to the big hangar. Only a few Langley Field officers were on hand to witness the test. The first test flight was just a short hop on which the plane did lift off and fly about half of the Langley Field long runway. Lieutenant Hamilton was not impressed with the plane and reported it was tail heavy. A series of wind-tunnel tests were conducted on the tail section in an attempt to rectify the problem.

On a later test flight an aileron cable broke while the plane was about 30ft (9.2m) off the ground, causing the wing to dip and the plane to drop as Lieutenant Hamilton attempted to slip it onto the runway. It hit hard enough to collapse the main gear and nosed over slightly. At first glance it did not appear to have been badly damaged, but the airframe had been twisted and sprung causing misalignments. It was reported that after the crash, Hamilton breathed a sigh of relief and walked away in disgust.

Johns now insisted that the Army resolve the matter one way or another, so the Air Service purchased the multiplane for one dollar. It was then repaired and some modifications were made during the winter months and a few more attempts were made to fly it, but it became obvious that major modifications would be needed. Rather than spend the time and

money, the Army abandoned the project and it was broken up in September 1920. Since it was never an

This closeup of the nose seems to be a Multiplane family portrait of the people connected with the project. The civilian on the sawhorse is thought to be Herbert Johns. The woman is unidentified but likely was connected with the firm, as is probably true of the two civilians on the ground. The officer to Johns' right may be Lt. Raymond W. Hamilton; he has three overseas hash marks on his left sleeve. Fred C. Dickey, Jr., Collection

official Army project and unsuccessful, it was allowed to simply fade away like an old soldier.

All Langley Field records were destroyed in a flood resulting from a 1933 hurricane, thus the following specifications were estimated.

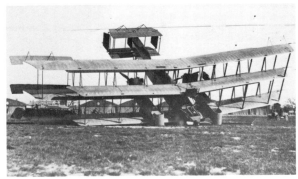

The Johns Multiplane augers in! As can be seen, the nose propeller has been broken, and the right nacelle damaged slightly. The landing gear cannot be seen, but obviously has been damaged too. Fred C. Dickey, Jr., Collection

Specifications:

Span 70–75ft (21.3–22.9m); length 50–55ft (15.2–16.8m); height 18–20ft (5.5–6.1m); empty weight 10,000lb (4,524.9kg). (Wingspan estimate is for triplane wings.)

Phillips Multiplane I

Another multiplane, in some ways similar to the Gerhard, was designed by Horatio F. Phillips in 1904. Phillips was a British engineer who became interested in the theory of lifting surface back before the turn of the century. He favored generating aerodynamic lift by using a series of winglets mounted one above another. His first multiplane had twenty winglets, a tricycle undercarriage, and a cruciform tail unit. He built his own engine and geared it to drive a wooden tractor propeller. During testing in 1904 at Streatham, while it developed adequate lift, it was difficult to control in flight. Phillips had designed and built what amounted to the first wind tunnel in 1880, and had conducted tests on hundreds of wing sections before determining that flat surfaces were useless for supporting weight in the air. In 1884 he patented a series of wing sections that he had proven would actually supply lift.

Another view of the crash, taken shortly after it occurred. The lower wing suffered some slight damage to the tip and aileron. The rear strut on the outside of the lower and middle wing has been splintered. And the tail wheels are missing; a skid was used for the test flights. Fred C. Dickey, Jr., Collection

His winglets were all hand carved out of yellow pine and were 19ft (5.8m) long but only an inch and a half wide. He carried on his experiments and in 1907 designed another "Venetian Blind," as his creations came to be called, with fifty winglets in four separate frames, the whole resembling a large box. This aircraft was a success as it flew a little over 500ft (152.4m). One design is reported to have had 100 winglets, though photographs of it are not to be found. Phillips was a fine engineer and unlike Gerhard, none of his winglet craft ever collapsed.

Sellers Quadruplane

Matthew Sellers continued to develop and improve his basic 1908 quadruplane glider as a powered airplane as late as 1929. What was probably his final effort was destroyed by fire at Roosevelt Field, New York, during an attempt to start the engine.

Unidentified American Multiwing

No record can be found to identify this one-of-a-kind American multiwing other than what can be determined by examining the photograph. The angle from which the photo was taken obscures many details. At first glance it appears to be a high-wing monoplane

This unknown late 1920s or early 1930s design with a full wing and four winglets remains a mystery ship. A Brunner-Winkle Bird biplane appears in the background. Bowers Collection

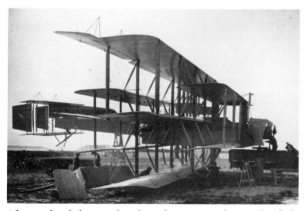

Aftermath of the crash. The salvage crew has righted the Johns and the extent of the damage to the aileron shows plainly. The center tractor propeller hub is exposed and the splintered strut has been removed. Lieutenant Hamilton did an excellent job of crash-landing with a bare minimum of visible damage. Bowers Collection

with a strut-braced wing mounted on top of a deep fuselage. Four short-span cantilever winglets are mounted in rearward descending order. Ailerons seem to be on only the upper wing. The landing gear is a standard type with a tail skid and wheels.

Judging by the unidentified seven-cylinder radial engine, metal propeller with its neat spinner, and the Brunner-Winkle Bird biplane in the background and the automobile in the right foreground, this plane would seem to have been built in 1930 or later, though it may have been designed a few years earlier.

Air Progress magazine ran a photo of a similar unknown design in its February/March 1965 issue, of a roadable plane featuring three pairs of stubby winglets: one set in front, another in a midship position, and a third at the rear with small vertical tail planes set in each winglet. The plane was apparently built in the 1930s and stored in a garage for twenty-five years. It was towed to the Cicero, New York, airport. Its Continental engine kicked over on the first attempt to start it. It had a bicycle landing gear and a tail wheel. The top winglets had squared-off wing tips, but the front and middle bottom winglets seem to have been designed to accept additional wing extensions. This seems logical because the winglets would not provide enough wing area to get it off the ground. Probably this aircraft could be called a tandem plane, if such was the case.

Chapter 8

Triplane Revival

As an airplane long considered passé, the triplane has made a remarkable comeback in recent years. It is safe to say that since 1957, more triplanes have been built or are presently under construction throughout the world than were built in all the years as far back as the end of World War I.

Only one of these modern projects, however, was a serious attempt at developing a specialized design for commercial use—the DeKellis-Olson Air Truck that was built to carry cargo to small towns, sawmills, and mines in the mountains surrounding Oroville, California, or to carry hunters and jeeps on charters.

Surprisingly, the other triplanes built since 1957 are neither new designs, nor are they intended for normal commercial or military use. They are mostly replicas of World War I single-seat fighters, with the German Fokker Dr.I being the most numerous, followed by the British Sopwith. Others, including a German Pfalz Dr.I, are known to be under construction at this writing.

Background of the Movement

In the United States the establishment of a recreational subcategory of the Experimental aircraft licensing category made the building and flying of homebuilt airplanes legal. In the official language, these are called Amateur-Built, and are for recreational use only. They cannot be flown for pay or rented out, and the builder must do 51 percent or more of the actual construction work on the plane. Those flown for compensation on Experimental-Exhibition licenses carry greater operating restrictions.

As a result of this new freedom, the nationwide (now worldwide) Experimental Aircraft Association (EAA) was formed in 1952. EAA provides organization, information exchange, interface with government regulatory organizations, and other services, for the still-growing movement. The parallel Antique Airplane Association (AAA) encourages the restoration of older production airplanes, some dating back to World War I.

Enter the Replica

In the absence of available World War I airplanes to restore, it was inevitable that nostalgic warplane buffs with the required skills would turn to building replicas of their favorite models. This is not all that hard to do. Good drawings and technical data for both the Fokker and Sopwith triplanes are readily available, and the structures are relatively simple and very similar to the modern homebuilts, particularly the Fokker with its welded-steel-tubing fuselage. Some of the Sopwiths are built with strict adherence to the wood and wire structures of the original, but as a timesaver, others are built with steel-tube fuselages.

Mention should be made here of the distinction between a "replica" and a "reproduction" airplane. Louis S. Casey, Curator of the National Air and Space Museum in Washington, D.C., stated that a replica could only be built by the organization that built the original. All others, even though built exactly to original factory drawings and using authentic vintage powerplants and equipment, must be called reproductions. In spite of his definition, the builders and their associated organizations call their projects replicas, and so do we.

Powerplant Problems

The major problem facing present-day builders of World War I replicas is finding a suitable powerplant. The old rotary and water-cooled static engines of the war years are extremely rare, there are no spare parts, and operation by current safety standards is extremely unreliable. A very few Fokker and Sopwith triplanes have been fitted with rotaries, but not necessarily the same model fitted to the original. Still, a rotary is a triumph in itself. The mechanical and operational problem of these engines rule them out for use in purely recreational replicas in the modern traffic environment.

Rotary-engine airplanes today have to be handled exactly as they were in their heyday. In those days, the plane did not have to taxi a long distance from the hangar to the end of a runway, hold for traffic, and then line up on the runway for takeoff. They were pushed to the starting line close to the hangar, pointed into the wind, started up, and then took off across a wide grassy field. After landing, if engine power was used to taxi back to the hangar, the services of wing-tip walkers were required. The rotary engine could not be idled for low-speed taxiing as it ran at nearly full throttle, and power was reduced by switching it off briefly. Help also was needed to hold the plane in check during the bursts of power, and the old airplanes had neither wheel brakes nor steerable tail wheels, so help was needed for slow-speed turning.

The majority of modern replicas use latter-day static radial engines, mostly 145–185hp Warner Scarabs or 220hp Continental R-670s as substitutes for rotaries. These fit well under the same cowlings and retain the authenticity of appearance while having the advantages of modern reliability, availability of replacement parts, and so on. These engines, plus steerable tail wheels and main wheels with brakes, allow such replicas to operate freely with general aviation airplanes in the modern environment.

Horsepower Discrepancy

Builders quickly learn that their replicas do not have the same performance of the originals. For one thing, most were considerably overweight, but this was not a serious handicap in itself. It turns out that the modern horsepower and the 1917 horsepower are simply not the same. The 110–120hp Oberursel or LeRhone had nine cylinders, a displacement of 919ci (15,066cc), a weight of 323lb (146.2kg), and turned an 8.5ft (2.6m) propeller 1200rpm. The 145hp Warner has seven cylinders, a displacement of 499ci (8,180cc), a weight of 305lb (138.0kg), and turns a 7ft (2.1m) propeller at a much less efficient 2050rpm. By the horsepower formula, the Warner is more powerful

than the 1917 rotary, but the old-timer delivers more thrust through its bigger and slower turning propeller.

Who Builds the Replicas?

Most replicas of World War I single-seaters are built by dedicated hobbyists and sport flyers as somewhat oversized equivalents of contemporary homebuilts, but are more slanted toward antiques than normal homebuilts. Their performance is generally similar to World War II biplane trainers like the Boeing/Stearman Kaydet. They are built entirely at the owner's expense and are operated as pure sport planes, with extensive participation in antique airplane or Warbirds fly-in gatherings. These operate with great freedom on their Experimental Amateur-Built licenses.

Others of a nonrecreational nature are built by professionals and by established specialty shops for profit to be flown at air shows, or for motion pictures or television productions. As such, they fly on the Experimental-Exhibition licenses. Others have been built on contract for aviation museums. These are externally and internally as accurate as possible, and feature original rotary engines. A few are flown briefly for exhibition or to prove their airworthiness, while others are simply put directly into the museum without ever flying.

One of the full-scale replicas of the 1910 Avro IV built for the movie Those Magnificent Men and Their Flying Machines. *The only upgrading of the design was the use of a 1928 rather* than a 1910 engine. Twentieth Century Fox via Frederick G. Freeman

A sight not seen since 1918—four Fokker Triplanes in the air together. These are four of the eight full-scale replicas that participated in the Aerodrome 92 air show at Guntersville, Georgia, on September 5–7, 1992. Ted Sacher

Avro Triplane—Film Star

In October 1963, a decision was reached to build three examples of each of five different 1910 airplanes for the Twentieth Century Fox movie, *Those Magnificent Men and Their Flying Machines*. The highlight of the film was to be an air race from Dover, England, to Paris, France. The movie was filmed in England. For the benefit of a nonaviation audience the five different airplanes had to be notably unique to enable the audience to identify each. This made the Avro IV triplane a logical choice. The reason for building three of each plane, even though only one would appear on the screen at a time, was to avoid costly filming delays if one was out of action due to a mechanical problem or even a crash.

The Avros were built by members of the Hampshire Aero Club. Design data was easy to obtain, and the wooden structure presented no problems or difficulties either. The original engine was a 35hp Green, a four-cylinder upright. A 1928 British Cirrus which was similar in appearance was used in lieu of the Green. Full power of the Cirrus was used only on takeoffs.

The one real oddity of the Avro for modern pilots was the wing warping system of lateral control. First flight of one took place on May 9, 1964, and subsequent operations were quite dependable. The surviving flying plane is now part of the Shuttleworth Collection and is on display at Old Warden Aerodrome, Biggleswade, Bedfordshire, England, where it is still flown on special occasions.

Replica Fokker Triplanes

Why should the Fokker triplane be the most popular model in the World War I replica airplane movement? There are several good reasons. One, a triplane is a thoroughly distinctive airplane without being a freak. Two, it has the charisma of the von Richthofen—Red Baron—legend and most seem to be painted all red. Three, it has a structure very similar to modern practices, and for full-scale replicas at least, can use the currently available engines without sacrificing authentic appearance.

Small Sorrell Fokkers

Surprisingly, the first Fokker Dr.I replicas were not built as part of the antique airplane craze, nor were they full-size replicas. They were three-quarter-scale airplanes intended to be homebuilts with a difference.

Hobart C. Sorrell of Rochester, Washington, was a long-time builder of unique homebuilt airplanes in the early days of the movement. He had a well-equipped shop, his own private grass airstrip, and a job that allowed him plenty of leisure time for his hobby.

He built his first Fokker in 1957, more or less as a whim. He had built a stack of ribs for another design he had in mind, but decided that he wanted a Fokker instead. All he had to go by was a very inaccurate three-view drawing in a book and some photos. The on-hand 65hp Continental A-65 engine, a small opposed or "flat-four" model, would not do for a full-scale model but would be suitable for a three-quarter-scale replica, and the existing ribs were the correct size. Three-quarters is a convenient size for an amateur builder. By the mathematical "cube law," bulk and weight vary as the cube of the dimension, so a three-quarter replica is only 42 percent as much airplane to build and is directly comparable to other homebuilts in the same power-to-weight class.

Reduced scale, however, introduces serious compromises with authenticity. The cockpits of World War I fighters were a tight fit for their pilots. However, a

Hobart C. Sorrell and his first three-quarter-scale Fokker Dr.I replica. Because of limited cockpit space, two of the flight instruments were built into the butts of the simulated machine guns. Bowers Collection

Side view of the three-quarter-scale Sorrell Fokker, showing the distorted proportions resulting from using a 65hp Continental A-65 engine, and the need to have a wider and deeper fuselage for the cockpit. This plane is now in the EAA Museum at Oshkosh, Wisconsin. Bowers Collection

three-quarter-size replica must still accommodate a full-size pilot, so the fuselage has to be out of scale in width and sometimes in depth to seat him. The nose also has to be longer when using a modern flat-four engine. The distance from the back of the propeller flange to the firewall is greater on the Continental or similar engine than a rotary, which has parts of its attachments inside the fuselage behind the firewall—

an installation impossible on current engines, flat or radial. Since the firewall on the replicas cannot be moved aft to absorb the difference, the nose must be notably longer than that on the original.

Sorrell avoided the complexity of the Fokker wing by using a single, solid spar with a plywood D-tube leading edge for the necessary torsional stiffness. Although his replica was three-fourth size, Sorrell kept

The second three-quarter-scale Sorrell Fokker, left, and the first of seven full-scale Dr.Is built by Walter Redfern (with
scarf). Careful spacing of the planes virtually eliminates the size discrepancy. Bowers Collection

First of the full-scale Fokker triplane replicas was built by Harry Provolt in 1958, using a cut-down fuselage from an existing plane. Note in this and the previous photo that the planes have small wheels built into the bottoms of the tail
skid, and that Redfern and Provolt used the latter-day 30x5.00in wheels with brakes for operation on paved runways. John Underwood Collection

the rudder full size to be sure of positive directional control. All of the accurate Fokker data that was heaped on Sorrell after his triplane appeared encouraged him to build another, more true to scale and powered by a 125hp Lycoming 0-290G flat-four engine.

Full-Size Fokker Triplanes

The first of the full-scale Fokker Dr.I replicas was built in 1958 by Harry Provolt, of Los Angeles, California, who used a 145hp Warner radial engine. Wing structure of necessity followed the original, but a shortcut was taken by using a cut-down steel-tube fuselage from an existing production airplane.

Many other recreational and exhibition Fokkers have been built since, but most have simplified and heavier fuselage structure that uses diagonal steel-tube braces rather than the original wires, and turnbuckles anchored by myriad welded-in steel corner loops. The popularity of the Fokker is well illustrated by the fact that eight of them were on hand for the World War I Aircraft Convention and Fly-in at Guntersville, Alabama, for the Aerodrome '92 event on September 5–7, 1992.

The only Fokker replica flying consistently with a rotary engine is the one built by Cole Palen of Poughkeepsie, New York, for use in his summer air

shows at the Old Reinbeck Aerodrome. This one has a 160hp Gnome engine, and the fuselage differs from standard in that the transition structure from the round firewall into the flat-sided fuselage is outside of the fabric rather than under it.

Commercial Production

Many of the flyable Fokkers have been built by commercial organizations for such professional operations as air shows, motion pictures, and television work. Perhaps the most viewed of the movie Fokkers are the three built by a German firm for the 1966 picture *The Blue Max*, powered by the Siemens-Halske Sh radial engines. These triplanes have been used in several other film productions.

Quite a few other nonflying Fokkers with flimsy construction and dummy engines have been built for display outside the 94th Aero Squadron restaurant chain, which features a World War I theme. They are usually paired with a Nieuport 28 of similar crude construction carrying the insignia of the 94th Aero Squadron, the famed "Hat-in-the-Ring."

Replica Sopwith Triplanes

These replicas are all full-scale aircraft. The first was built in 1970 from Sopwith factory drawings by

The only Fokker Dr.I replica flown regularly with a rotary engine is this one built by Cole Palen for his air show. The engine is a 160hp Gnome, which was used in the French Nieu- port 28 flown by the American Expeditionary Force in 1918. John Doyle

155

professional builder Carl Swanson of Sycamore, Illinois, and is powered by a 130hp Clerget. Color and markings are those of Canadian Ace Raymond Collishaw's (sixty victories) *Black Maria*. Collishaw scored thirty victories flying it. The replica triplane was flown briefly and then retired to the Canadian National Aviation Museum at Rockcliffe Airport, Ottawa, Ontario, Canada.

The second flyable Sopwith was built by professional builder Ed Marquart of Riverside, California. It is also in Collishaw's markings and has a steel-tube fuselage and a 145hp Warner engine.

One of the three Fokker replicas built for the movie The Blue Max. *The crosses on the wing are incorrect, and the lozenge-pattern fabric was never used on the Dr.I. These are typical* errors seen on many replicas and display airplanes. *Twentieth Century Fox via Frederick G. Freeman*

One of the several nonflying replica Fokker triplanes built as an outdoor attraction for a national restaurant chain featuring a World War I theme—though this one appears to be in an auto dealer's lot. Naturally, it is all-red. *Arthur P. Dowd*

First of the Sopwith triplane replicas, built by Carl Swanson for the Canadian National Aviation Museum. It was flown briefly and is fitted with a Clerget rotary engine. *Walter J. Addems*

Carl Swanson, now of Darien, Wisconsin, built another Sopwith, in just twenty-two months and delivered it in 1984 to the Champlin Fighter Museum in Mesa, Arizona. The Clerget engine was assembled from parts of two 130hp rotaries. It is accurate in every detail and carries the markings of Sub-Lieutenant Mel Alexander's *Black Prince*. He scored five victories with it, and later added thirteen more while flying a Camel. He was a member of Naval No. 10's "Black Flight."

The Numbers Grow

As the popularity of the homebuilt airplane grows in the face of rising costs of production airplanes and the discontinuance of many of the smaller private-owner and training types by the industry worldwide, replicas as well as homebuilts continue to be built. World War I Aero, 15 Crescent Road, Poughkeepsie, New York, a nonprofit enthusiast's organization, keeps track of all the existent original and replica World War I airplanes.

Many Fokker Dr.Is are either completed or under construction at this writing, December 1992. If the present rate of proliferation continues, there may soon be more replica Fokker Dr.Is in the world than were built in 1917–1918.

As long as replica airplanes can continue to be built and flown by enthusiastic hobbyists, the triplane will hold its place by simply being what it is: a romantic anachronism with a notable difference that alone is enough to justify its continued existence in the modern air world.

DeKellis-Olson Triplane: The Last Triplane

The honor of being the last original triplane designed and built goes to the DeKellis-Olson Air Truck designed and built by Thomas E. DeKellis and Alan Olson of Oroville, California. DeKellis was a pilot who lived in Wyandotte, California, and was an operator and instructor at the Oroville Municipal Airport for nine years before branching out into crop dusting. He soon decided to obtain an airplane better suited for the job. Failing to find the ideal plane he decided to build one himself, teaming up with Alan Olson, a mechanic who had attended Cal-Aero Technical Institute after the war.

DeKellis wanted a light plane with high maneuverability and increased carrying capacity, and was

This Sopwith replica built by Ed Marquart was intended for consistent flight in the modern environment, and features a Warner radial engine in a lengthened nose with a steerable *tail wheel in lieu of the tail skid. The fuselage is welded-steel tubing instead of wood and wire.* John Underwood Collection

Carl Swanson also built this replica Sopwith for the Champlin Fighter Museum in Mesa, Arizona, at Falcon Field. He assembled the Clerget from parts of two others. It took twenty-two months to build. Col. J. Ward Boyce

Cockpit of the Champlin Fighter Museum's Black Prince, *showing the excellent attention to detail and workmanship of Carl Swanson.* Col. J. Ward Boyce

fully aware that no aircraft was ever designed expressly for crop dusting. Deciding on a triplane configuration, DeKellis and Olson spent two years gathering parts from four different airplanes because they figured that by using proven components, they would save thousands of dollars in testing and installation. The first full-size plans were laid out on a hangar floor after chalking the outlines of a Jeep—they started thinking in terms of possible use as a cargo carrier as well as a crop duster.

DeKellis then filled in the balance of the dimensions after he worked them out on a scale model. He knew the problem was not to just get the plane to fly with a bulky or heavy load, but to get it to land and take off in a short field. While the plane would weigh about 3,000lb (1,357.5kg) empty, he wanted it to carry at least 3,000lb of payload. For utility's sake they used a box-like fuselage with a wide-opening cargo door at the rear. The cargo compartment could accommodate a Jeep. The tail was mounted on twin booms to enable the cargo doors to swing open for loading and unloading

ease. The booms were attached to the upper part of the fuselage.

The problem of good pilot visibility—a crucial item for a crop duster—was solved in a unique manner, by putting the pilot and cockpit up next to the 450hp Pratt and Whitney engine. The engine was set more than a foot off center to allow room for the pilot's seat. The offset engine was to be compensated for by trimming the ship for flight and the torque of the turning propeller offset most of the unbalanced engine thrust. The lift provided by the three wide wings enabled the Air Truck to take off in a very short space. Slow landing speed of 65–70mph allowed it to land in a small field, an important factor for a crop duster, which must land, reload, and get back in the air fast from whatever landing fields are available. The working speed was to be 20mph (32.2km/h) slower than conventional dusting planes.

Flaps to further slow the plane were incorporated into the ailerons. A vertical fin called a spill plate was placed at the wing tip of each wing to lend more stability at low flying speeds. The twin tails with the twin rudders also furnished better control at lower speeds. The three wings had a lot of positive stagger. Loaded, the plane flew at an angle of attack that had the top and middle wing acting as a slot to smooth out the airflow past the bottom wing which, in turn, reduced the stalling speed. The top wing also had a full-length slot on the upper leading edge to accomplish the same purpose.

The wings were fabric covered. It had a four-wheel landing gear like a truck. It logged at least seven hours of flying time in 1957, and the designers felt it would have many applications besides dusting. They felt it could be used to haul cargo to sawmills and mines, as well as for mountain flying, and for charter flights for fishing and hunting trips to remote locations. It eventually was disassembled and put in storage. Its final fate is unknown.

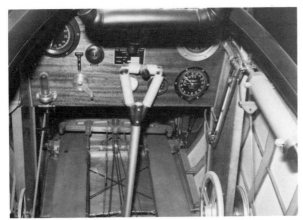

Excellent closeup of the interior of the Sopwith at the Champlin Museum. Col. J. Ward Boyce

The DeKellis-Olson Air Truck on the Oroville strip on August 2, 1958. It was still on the Federal Aviation Administration (FAA) register of January 1967 with N-2851D, FAA code 056- *GW, and was listed as constructor number AT-1.* B. C. Reed via William T. Larkins

Scale-model triplanes are common enough in the model world, but there are also triplanes in the nonscale free-flight category. Snoopy finally gets his chance to meet the Bloody Red Baron, one on one, triplane versus triplane. Note the *snarl on Snoopy's lips. It looks bad for the Baron. Some credit must be given to old Snoopy for helping to revive the triplane's popularity.* Warren D. Shipp Collection

Index